Bowhunting
The West & Beyond

Scott Haugen
Foreword by Dwight Schuh

SHOOT STRAIGHT!
Scott H—

Dedication

To my two sons, Braxton and Kazden, and my wonderful wife, Tiffany. During those long days when I'm away from home, you're constantly in my thoughts and prayers. Your continued support and unconditional love have allowed me to live a life many men only dream of, and for that I am forever grateful.

Published by:
Haugen Enterprises
2010, Springfield, OR

Softbound ISBN-13: 978-0-9819423-2

All photographs taken by the author unless otherwise noted.
www.scotthaugen.com

Book and cover design by Tony Amato

Printed in Singapore

1 3 5 7 9 10 8 6 4 2

Contents

Acknowledgments

Were it not for the help of others, I wouldn't be writing these words today. True, I've gotten to where I am through hard work and dedication, but if it weren't for many folks providing direction and influencing me along the way, I'd likely not be sharing these, some of my most coveted bowhunting adventures.

In 1997 I wrote my first magazine article and haven't looked back. Since that time I've penned over 1,200 stories for numerous magazines around the world. None of that would have been possible were it not for the support of many editors–too many to name.

On the television front, there are the people at Wolf Creek Productions, Media Jungle and the Outdoor Channel. Were it not for their support, encouragement and the opportunities they've presented me with, few of the hunts within these pages would have materialized.

To all the outfitters, guides and land owners who've allowed me to hunt with them over the years, I sincerely thank you. Your generosity has been the reason why I've enjoyed so many fine hunts.

Within the bowhunting industry, the folks at SportHill clothing, BowTech and Gold Tip deserve a very special thank you. Without your support, wisdom and cutting edge technology and equipment, I would not be where I am today.

Finally, to my parents Jerry and Jean Haugen. Thanks for teaching me so much about the outdoors at such an early age, and for all you continue to do to help my family both when I'm on the road and around home. Without you, I don't know where I'd be in life.

Thanks to all of you for motivating me to live the dream, and more importantly, share these experiences which I hold so close to my heart.

Introduction

I'll never forget the looks on everyones faces when I told them I'd just taken a bird with my bow. It was Thanksgiving day, 1968 and we had a house full of relatives, most of whom were avid hunters.

"That's great, Scotty, good job," they muttered over the blare of the football game, never taking their eyes off the television. I tried explaining, "But, it's a house sparrow, and they're really...."

"Uh huh, nice," someone said.

I was crushed. I was only four years old, but it hurt that no one else wanted to share in the jubilation of my success. After all, house sparrows, though they were a menace, were not easy to get with a bow, especially for a four year old boy.

I went out on the back porch and held the bird in my hand, trying to decide what to do. I took it around the house and held it up to the front window, where everyone was watching TV.

When my dad saw it, his face lit-up. He couldn't get out of his chair fast enough, and came outside to congratulate me. Together, we sat on the front porch and talked about how the hunt had unfolded. By this young age I'd been with Dad on some of his successful deer and waterfowl hunts, and was hooked on hunting.

Though that little hunt took place in the orchard behind our countryside home, it planted a bowhunting seed within me, one that continues to grow, even today. Since then I've been blessed to hunt many exciting places around the globe, and have seen things I'd otherwise never have known to exist were it not for the hunting that took me there.

I'm not one to climb a mountain simply to enjoy a view, or cross a river to see what's on the other side. But if there's an animal to hunt, I'll go anywhere, anytime.

I'm not the greatest hunter in the woods and don't pretend to be, but like many outdoorsmen, I give it my best shot every time I'm in the field. Personally, I feel there are no experts when it comes to hunting, for when pursuing wild animals the variables are continually changing, meaning one never masters all there is to know about the animals or nature. That's what I love so much about hunting and being outdoors; the learning process is never-ending.

My involvement with athletics kept me from getting too involved with bowhunting during my high school and college years. Being a four-sport letterman at Thurston High School, and playing a bit of college football required a great deal of time. But the discipline and drive I learned through athletics have helped pave the way for what I feel has been a successful bowhunting career thus far in my life.

After high school I attended the University of Oregon, where I majored in geography, minored in biology and earned a Masters degree in education. After 12 years of teaching science, most of which was spent in two tiny, extremely remote Inupiat Eskimo villages on the North Slope of Alaska–followed by four years in the jungle of Sumatra, Indonesia–I entered into the field of outdoor writing.

Since penning my first magazine article in 1997, and having jumped into the outdoor industry full-time in 2000, I never looked back. The harder I worked, the more opportunities presented themselves. Before I knew it, I was writing for more than 40 hunting and fishing magazines around the world, started writing books, delivering seminars and dabbling in outdoor television.

In the fourth grade I began running my own trapping line. When my wife, Tiffany, and I moved to Alaska, the trapping continued. There I regularly trapped wolves, wolverine, lynx and more. The trapping and hunting I continued to partake in during my early years taught me a great deal about how to read animals, survive in the outdoors and more; stuff I couldn't learn in any other way than by being in the woods.

In the mid '90s I stepped-up my bowhunting efforts. By this time I'd rifle hunted many places around the globe, and became more intrigued with the challenges and growing opportunities that bowhunting presented.

As my writing career continued to blossom, the prospects of getting more serious about bowhunting intrigued me. Along the way I received help from various archers and pro shops, to all of whom I'm grateful. But where I really started learning the

6

intricacies of bowhunting was when I jumped in with both feet and dedicated myself to the sport.

The more time I spent in the woods, the more I learned, and continue to learn. Often my mind slips back to that sparrow I arrowed when I was four years old. Now, like that time in 1968, I often find myself alone in the woods, with no one to celebrate the filling of a tag with. That's fine, and I can accept that, as I like doing most things alone when it comes to the world of hunting, especially bowhunting.

Compared to many bowhunters, my career is short-lived. But since the mid '90s I've learned a lot, and taken some beautiful animals. To date, more than 30 of the animals I've arrowed would qualify for various record books of the world, but I've never chosen to enter them. To me, personally, the hunt isn't about seeing my name in a record book or becoming famous. My reward comes in outsmarting mature animals, capturing the thrills for television and being able to communicate with others what I learned in the process.

What I've come to love most about bowhunting are the mental and physical demands it places on me. Not since my trapping days did I have to think so much like the animals, even behave like them in order to find success. Bowhunting pushes a hunter to the highest level of performance, and when success comes, spurs what could be the greatest natural high a person can experience. It's something non-bowhunters can't fully relate to until they live it, firsthand.

I'm sometimes ridiculed for being too excited when I take an animal on TV. That's the real me, and when that enthusiasm leaves my heart it will be time for me to find another profession.

The more I got into bowhunting, the more things changed, quickly. As I gained more hunting experience around the world, more and more magazine writing assignments came my way. Television also made its way into my life.

Before I knew it, I was asked to guest host a few shows for Cabela's as well as Wolf Creek Productions. Wolf Creek Productions then offered me a job hosting my own show, and things forever changed. Without that support I would not be where I am today.

Soon, BowTech became the title sponsor of my show, and this allowed me to travel to many places in search of exciting bowhunting adventures. Then I moved on to hosting various shows on the Outdoor Channel, namely Adventures Abroad and Outdoor America.

Then another hosting opportunity presented itself, and things just kept getting better. Jim Burnworth, owner of Media Jungle, was producing two shows for the Outdoor Channel when he called and asked if I'd like to host a third show for him. I accepted, and together we launched Game Chasers.

The world of outdoor writing and television is a volatile one, and constantly changing, so I never really know where I'll be or what I'll be doing from one year to the next. The one thing I do know: I have no intentions of slowing down or leaving the world of hunting.

For me, the greatest rewards of what I do come in being able to share my experiences with others. My two goals through TV, writing and seminars are to educate and motivate. If I can teach people something about the animals I hunt, and motivate them to get outdoors, I'm happy.

On average I spend over 200 days a year in the field–be it hunting, fishing, scouting or photographing wildlife–and learn something every time I'm out there. In my efforts to share what I learn, I pen over 100 stories for magazines each year, try and write a book or two, and film nearly 30 hunts, annually.

My wife, now a full-time stay-at-home mom, also writes cookbooks. She delivers cooking seminars and totally runs our family business. Our lifestyle is not normal, nor is it easy, but we love it. We always say, "We'd rather work 18 hours a day for ourselves than 8 for someone else." Until God or our two sons, Braxton and Kazden, tell us otherwise, we'll keep leading this hectic but rewarding lifestyle.

In the pages that follow, it's my goal to bring some of my most memorable hunts to life and teach a little something along the way. Some of the success stories capture what I did right to help fill a tag, and relay what I did wrong, for that's how one truly learns, by making mistakes. I'll also reveal what it's really like to film hunts for outdoor television, and relay the true pressures, frustrations and joys that come with that.

I truly hope that everyone who picks up this book learns something to help make them a better bowhunter. At the very least, I hope the stories take you into my world, and motivate you to one day experience some of these hunts for yourself.

It's a blessed world we live in and hunting is the perfect catalyst to take us places we otherwise may never go. I can't imagine life without hunting, or being able to share what I've learned from it. It's a big world, with more hunting opportunities than can be experience in a lifetime. Don't put off those hunts, get out and live the dream.

Scott Haugen

Foreword

What bowhunter doesn't love the prospect of adventure; of hunting far corners of the world; of pursuing horned, antlered, and furry big game of all sizes and attitudes; of exploring territory rarely, if ever, seen by other human beings?

That would describe most of us. But for most of us that prospect remains only a dream, a longing in our minds and hearts. Not for Scott Haugen. Scott is one of the fortunate few among us smart enough, driven enough, and energetic enough to live out his hunting dreams.

As many of us do, Scott got his early spark for hunting as a young boy while following his father through the fields and forests, hunting small game around his home and running a trapline. That early background planted an inherent love for the outdoors and hunting in his heart.

Although high school and college sports temporarily interrupted his hunting, Scott's next step in life jump-started it in a big way. After earning his Master's degree in education, Scott taught school in far corners of the earth – remote villages of Alaska, followed by four years in Sumatra, Indonesia – where he saw and lived at the Earth's cultural, environmental, and wildlife extremes. These experiences truly gave him a worldwide perspective.

Perhaps this perspective helped pave the way for the remainder of his life as he ended his 12-year teaching career and launched a new career in the world of hunting and outdoor communication. As Scott began selling magazine stories, publishing his own outdoor books, presenting hunting seminars, and hosting TV programs, he earned the opportunity to visit many other far corners of the world.

His writing and TV ventures have taken him from Alaska to Africa, Canada to New Zealand, in pursuit of elk, moose, bears, pronghorn antelope, blacktail deer, numerous species of African game, and many other big game species coveted by all hunters. Talk about a worldwide perspective! Not only will most of us never see and do firsthand what Scott has seen and done; we cannot even dream that big.

Perhaps most amazingly, no rich benefactor has handed Scott these opportunities. Nor has Scott earned wealth in business, medicine, the legal profession, or widget sales to afford him the luxury of buying adventures without regard for money. Nor has he simply got lucky. No, Scott Haugen is a guy who has had the vision, the smarts, and the determination to formulate his own big dreams – and to live them out.

Yes, Scott Haugen is one of those unique individuals who developed a love for hunting as a young boy, filled his heart and mind with big game hunting dreams, and truly brought his dreams to life as an adult. If you're one of those hunters who longs for hunting adventure, follow Scott Haugen in *Bowhunting the West & Beyond*, as he takes you to far corners of the world in pursuit and fulfillment of adventure. No doubt his writing will satisfy and fulfill some of your own dreams and longings. Better yet, it may very well inspire you to bring your own hunting dreams to fruition.

—*Dwight Schuh*
Editor, *Bowhunter* Magazine

Chapter 1:

Backcountry Bulls

When it comes to bowhunting out West, Wyoming offers numerous opportunities. This is especially true for elk, and what better place to live out one of North America's best backcountry hunts than in the famed Absaroka Range?

When the draw results finally appeared on the computer screen, a "yes" popped-up beneath the "successful" column. I was elated, for I'd just drawn a Wyoming elk tag.

Months of working out in the weight room, running and hiking with a full pack passed and before I knew it I was sliding into a saddle, on my way up the mountain in search of elk. I was with good friends, Tom Buller and Bob Wells, both Wyoming residents. Tom and I had been friends since we were in diapers, yet due to our changing lives hadn't hunted together for over 30 years. Since we'd be hunting the wilderness on our own, Tom registered with the Game and Fish department which allowed me to hunt under his supervision, without a registered guide.

It was the first time either Tom or Bob had been into this remote setting, 18 miles from where we parked the horse trailer. The higher we rode to our 10,000-foot level campsite in the Absaroka Range, east of Yellowstone National Park, the more prominent elk sign became. Grizzly tracks were everywhere, a reminder that we were entering an area with the highest bear densities in the Lower 48.

Upon our arrival at camp, old wallows and numerous rubs left no doubt elk had used the area–the question was, were they still around? A light skiff of snow fell the first night, making for perfect hunting conditions. The next day appeared promising, but there were no elk to be found, only grizzlies.

A severe snowstorm kept us locked in the tent for the next day-and-a-half, and when it finally subsided, we emerged from the tent only to find ourselves, and our horses, knee-deep in snow. A storm warning was in effect, and given how rapidly the powder accumulated at the high elevation, we had no choice but to pull out with the next break in the weather.

Dropping off the mountain was depressing. For years we'd planned this November rifle hunt, and now it was coming to an abrupt end. Even our backup spots were laden in snow, making access impossible.

I'd leave Wyoming with a tag in my pocket and bitter memories of how unforgiving backcountry elements can be. But what we'd seen on that trip planted a seed of optimism in our minds, and hope for the future. The array of rubs and wallows left no question elk were in the region during the rut, meaning targeting the bulls in archery season might be a smarter choice.

A few months later, there I was again, eyes pasted to the computer, anxiously anticipating Wyoming's elk drawing results. This time my heart sank as the word "no" appeared beneath the "successful" column. Tom and Bob, being Wyoming residents, purchased their tags over-the-counter and headed into the same area as the year prior, this time with their bows in hand.

While I was chasing elk in Oregon's backcountry, I couldn't help but wish I was high in the Wyoming wilderness, watching those rubs and wallows being made. Due to work commitments, Tom and Bob had only one day to hunt, but still made the long haul into the mountains, right where we'd camped the previous year.

On opening morning, September 1st, Tom had a 350-inch class bull come within bow range, but a clear shot never presented itself. Bob was more fortunate, taking a 320-inch bull with one well-placed arrow. Heading down the mountain, both men agreed it was the best action they had seen and were already making plans for next season. The bulls were responding well to cow calls, and bugles were heard throughout the valley all day long.

The following year, there I was again staring at my computer screen in the middle of winter, anticipating what the fall may bring. Bingo! A "yes" appeared under the "successful" column; I couldn't get to the phone fast enough. At that moment, Tom, Bob and I began making plans for our early season archery expedition, a hunt that would play out even better than expected.

Eighteen miles on horseback got my buddies and I in to our Wyoming wilderness elk camp.

The day we saddled-up the string of horses, the thermometer registered nearly 80 degrees, less than ideal elk hunting conditions. Following an 18 mile ride to the same camp location where we were forced out by snow on my first hunt, this time we were greeted by blue skies, fresh wallows and impressive rubs.

Arriving in camp two days before the season opener, we wanted to allow ample time to locate bulls. Within a few hours, it became evident the added days were not necessary. As we tied-off the tent and hoisted our food out of grizzly reach, it was mid-afternoon and bulls were steadily talking.

Less than 300 yards from camp a lone bull let out a bugle, followed by another bull in the canyon below. Throughout the night elk bugled; we got little sleep. The action continued well into morning and it was obvious there was no need to go looking for elk, we had found them. Sticking tight to camp, all we could do was wait until the next day, the season opener.

Up and ready to go before daybreak, we fed and watered the horses, then secured them for the day. Given the threat of grizzlies, we surrounded the horses with a portable electric fence, not only to keep grizzlies out, but the horses in. The moment we left camp we were hunting.

Working our way to the edge of a draw, the first elk seen was a nice 5x5. Little did we know at the time, but he'd be the smallest bull we'd see the entire trip; nonetheless, he was worth trying for. I stayed high on the ridge while Tom and Bob worked into shooting position. Though the five point didn't show any interest in our cow calls, two 6x6s did. From the west end of the draw a dandy six-point worked his way to the call. He was soon joined by another, hot six-pointer. They met head-on, sized-up one other, did some sparring, then resumed feeding up the opposite hillside.

Farther up the valley another bull responded to our calls. Though this, the third six-point of the morning, didn't come into range, things were looking good. We'd been hunting less than an hour and three of the four bulls we'd seen were record-class animals.

Choosing to cross the deep canyon and hit the heavy timber on the opposite ridge, our efforts would be rewarded. We were now four miles from base camp with no sign of humans and elk bugling everywhere.

Wallows were prevalent in every draw, and in places there were more rubbed trees than ones left unscathed. The stench of rutting elk hung heavy in the forest, and trails etched deep into the peat revealed just how long this area had been used by the mountain monarchs.

The hike into the area was mentally and physically grueling, which explained why we had it to ourselves. At times we were even hesitant to shoot anything should an opportunity present itself, for concern of not being able to get the horses near the downed prizes. By 10:00 a.m. we'd reached our desired area.

By noon, several bulls had responded to our calls, though seeing them in the thick forest was tough. Then a raspy bugle of a mature bull resonated from a nearby draw. Though he answered every cow sound Bob made, he was not coming in. Attempting to stalk within range, I got the jitters the moment I saw the colossal 370-class bull. I'd get close to bow range three different times, but no shot presented itself. When I finally had him at 35 yards, I thought it was a done deal. The massive bull flailed in a wallow, covering his body in gray mud, urinating and bugling in glory about his existence in this lush valley.

The only thing separating us was a small, three-foot tall pine tree. All the bull had to do was stand, step to one side and it was over. I was in no rush, simply waiting for the bull to make a move. Several minutes elapsed and the bull hadn't budged; that's when I got impatient and made a mistake. Rather than waiting, I gave him a light cow call. He

16

didn't even raise his head to acknowledge my sound, but seconds later a 330-class 6x6 charged in and stood less than 10 yards from me.

Though the six point was a nice bull, he was nothing like the giant below me, still wallowing in the muddy hole of his rich, green hideaway. Then the newcomer winded me and busted out of there, taking small trees and branches as he fled. It sounded like a locomotive and the commotion alerted the big bull. He wasted no time reacting. Tossing back his head, the bull rambled up the adjacent hillside, the ends of his ivory-tipped rack rubbing against his rump patch as he melted into the trees. It was the last time I ever saw him.

Dejected at having been so close, yet not closing the deal on such a fine animal, I was at a loss for words. Bob, in his always positive spirits, suggested we keep moving.

In less than 10 minutes we were set up once again, calling into a timbered draw. Immediately a bugle came back–the bull was close. I'll never forget the sounds of this heavy-chested bull as he came in on the run. His chest cavity resonated with gasps and grunts as he made his way down the steep hillside, directly at us.

The echoing of cracking branches left no doubt the bull meant business, and before I could reach full-draw, the bull was on me, six yards away, his wet, coal-black nose pumping the air to detect what we were. His ears worked hard, the whites of his eyes glistening as they rolled back in his head. He was fully alert, and knew something wasn't right.

The moment the 340-inch bull bolted, Bob hit him with a cow call. As the bull stopped, I drew while simultaneously finding the mark on his chest that I wanted the broadhead to hit. It happened fast, and I distinctly recall seeing the tufted top of a young pine tree only a few yards in front of me. Adjusting my hold, I let the arrow fly. Unfortunately, I failed to adjust my hold enough.

My broadhead struck the very tip of that little tree, sending the arrow into the dirt between the bull's legs. My second bonehead mistake in less than 15 minutes on two exceptional bulls, crushed my spirit.

We still had two hours before heading back to camp. Working our way around the next ridge, we were soon calling again. At the sound of Bob's first hyper cow call, three bulls simultaneously responded. The one high on the ridge sounded most intense, and a few more cow calls got him riled.

At first the bull stood his ground, not wanting to leave. But the seductive cow talk got the best of him and 10 minutes later the

Bob Wells was first to fill his tag on this impressive bull...
but the others came shortly after.

bull came trotting down through the brush, presenting an ideal broadside shot. Bob had a window and took it, perfectly placing his arrow at 40 yards.

Moments later, while we were waiting for Bob's bull to expire, the sound of raking antlers caught our attention. We were so focused on Bob's bull, we'd forgotten about the other two bulls in the area.

Glancing around a grove of young pines, the top of one tree whipped about with reckless abandon, only 50 yards away. A subtle cow call further enraged the bull, and when he was done stripping the young tree of all its branches, he grew intent on our sounds. At 23 yards the bull stared straight over my shoulder, fixed on Bob's calling. Bringing my bow to full-draw, I held the 20 yard pin square on the bull's chest. Then I let down.

The bull ran off and I turned to Bob. "Why didn't you shoot?" he whispered. "He was barely 300-inches," was my reply.

We had a quick chat about how exceptional this place was, sporting big bulls around every corner. Then Bob reminded me that a 300-inch bull, with a bow, is something most hunters would give anything to shoot.

"Okay, if you can call that bull back in, I'll take him," I smiled at Bob, halfway hoping it wouldn't happen.

Up to the challenge, Bob let loose with a series of excited cow sounds. I couldn't believe my ears when the sounds of crashing brush and snapping limbs grew louder as they came our direction. Seconds later, there was the bull, again, back for another look.

As promised to Bob, I prepared for the shot. When the bull broke through a stand of eight-foot tall pines, I could barely see him silhouetted against the afternoon sun which now hung low on the mountain tops. I tried putting my sight pin on the bull, but the glaring sun clogged my peep. Bob sensed what was happening, and called again.

The bull moved forward while working to my left. A few more steps and the sun wouldn't be a factor. Now all I needed was an opening, and for the bull to stop in it. As he skirted to the side, I tracked him with my 40 yard pin, then my 30. Then, at 28 yards he turned into an opening and Bob stopped him with a quick chirp.

Putting the pin on the bull's chest, the arrow hit the mark, and the bull was off. Listening to the bull's death run, a resounding crash echoed through the calm, evening air. No question, the bull had expired on the run, less than 50 yards from where he'd been hit.

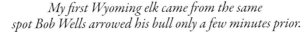

My first Wyoming elk came from the same spot Bob Wells arrowed his bull only a few minutes prior.

With two bulls down, now the work began. Snapping photos of my prized 6x6, we had it quartered and hanging high in the trees in good time. Moving on to Bob's bull, we began taking photos, then a lone bull bugled below us. Another bull in the timber above answered. Bob responded with his own bugle and the two bulls fired right back. A quick cow call triggered another response, and Tom barely had time to grab the bow and get into position.

Sprinting into a small clearing, Tom hadn't been there a minute when the bull arrived from above. Breaking into the clearing, the massive, wide-sweeping rack surprised all of us. At 16 yards Tom's

My boyhood friend, Tom Buller, scored big on this 340-class bull to put an amazing end to one of the best days of elk hunting a trio of friends could ask for.

The last trip to the pack horses found us relishing in a fresh, mountain waterfall.

As long as cows are around this time of year, bulls won't be far.

shot was perfect and the 340-class, seven-point bull went down 40 yards from where he was hit.

Within a 300 yard radius we had three record book bulls down and our work cut out for us. Fortunately, we were able to walk the horses near the kills, where butchering commenced the following morning. On our last trip to the horses, we each carried the heads and capes of our bulls. Passing by a small waterfall, we paused, drank from our filtered water bottles, showered, and prepared for the hours of hiking ahead.

The good part, we were able to load our packstring with all three bulls as well as our entire camp. The bad part, there was no room for us to ride. We had no choice but to walk the 22 miles from the kills, back to the trailhead. The temperatures were hot, and our number one priority was to get the meat off the mountain before it spoiled.

Heading out of the hills was a good feeling, and the fact we had three great bulls in tow only added to the jubilation. In all we covered 58 miles–22 on horseback, 36 on foot. While the do-it-yourself, wilderness country adventure was painful, demanding work, it was also one of the most rewarding hunts of our lives.

Staggering back to the horse trailers, we unsaddled the packstring and downed several bottles of water. Our bodies, aching in pain, would slowly recover. Nonetheless, right then and there plans were made for our next hunt into this unforgettable land of the big bulls...and there would be a next time.

Chapter 2:

Halloween Muley

A true icon of the West, the mule deer is one of bowhunting's greatest animals to pursue. The varied habitat in which they live, and their seasonal shifts in behavior, make them an ever-changing challenge. On this hunt, I got more than one slice of humble pie, then Halloween rolled around.

Crawling up to the edge of a vertical cliff, I could clearly see a few does feeding below me. Because they were across a draw, on an opposing grassy knoll, their distance was greatly reduced. Checking with my rangefinder, I was surprised when it read 72 yards–it seemed much farther than that.

I knew the buck was below the does, not yet in sight from my elevated vantage point. We'd spotted him from across the canyon, nearly a mile from where I now sat. It was late October, and the rut was on in this little corner of South Dakota.

When the does put their heads down to feed, I inched closer to the edge of the cliff, trying to contain my wincing as cacti spikes were driven into my knees. Arrow nocked, I knew the buck was near and didn't want to blow it, not after the long stalk I'd put in.

Finally, as I peered through a tuft of dry, golden grass, I could see the buck's back. Then he lifted his head. The rangefinder registered 65 yards, and compensating for the extreme downhill angle, I figured holding my 50 yard pin low on the buck's vitals would be perfect. I was wrong.

The moment I touched the release, I knew the arrow was sailing high. I could have easily placed my 30 yard pin on the spot and connected. What I would have given to have one of the fancy rangefinders with a built-in inclinometer, a tool that hadn't yet hit the market.

I was flustered, to say the least, as I'd just blown the chance on a 165-inch 4x4. Several thoughts raced through my mind, not the least of which was all the time and effort I'd put in to preparing for this hunt.

I shoot my bow year-round, and work-out lifting weights, running, hiking and/or biking at least five days a week, all for the sake of staying in shape for the hunt. I'd been shooting my bow very well, and felt certain the buck was mine the minute I settled my 50 yard pin on him.

When shooting on the range in my backyard, I routinely practice at 70, 80 and 90 yards. Being able to consistently hit the spot at these ranges, makes taking those average 40 yard shots much easier. Western bowhunters are often chastised for our long-range shooting, but with today's state-of-the-art, high-speed bows and solid practice sessions, making such shots are doable for some people.

I once read a report that the average shot distance for whitetail deer entered into the record books was 17 yards. The same report claimed the average shot distance for mule deer entered into the books was 41 yards.

I'm not saying nor am I advocating that everyone should, or could, shoot long range, as that's up to each individual to decide for themselves. It all comes down to natural abilities, shooting skills, the equipment and how much quality practice time you put in. When I first started bowhunting, my effective range was 30 yards. Over the years, as I've honed my shooting skills and logged valued practice hours, my effective range has dramatically increased.

When it comes time to decide whether or not to take a long shot, or any shot, certain factors must be taken into consideration. The most important of these, for me, is to observe how the animal is behaving. If the animal is relaxed, not wired and looking like he'll react to the shot (jump the string), then I check the wind. Not only do I look at the wind where I'm shooting from, but also at where the animal is and all the land separating us. If the wind is too strong, making it tough to hold steady, or if I feel the wind will carry my arrow too far off-course, then I'll wait.

If the animal is calm and I'm comfortable with the wind, then feel steady once I reach full-draw, I'll take the shot. Of these three factors, the animal's behavior is the ultimate decision maker on whether or not I take any shot, be it long or short-range.

On the buck I'd just missed, it was my fault, not that of my equipment. Fortunately, there were plenty of deer around, as is always the case in that particular game-rich area.

I was with good friend and outfitter, Reese Clarkson, owner of Mill Iron Outfitters situated in the northwest corner of South Dakota, just north of the tiny town of Buffalo. Over the years I've hunted many times with Reese, and we've filmed several TV shows together.

On this hunt, we were filming an episode of BowTech's Western Adventures, a show I was hosting on the Men's Channel. I love hunting with Reese and spending time with his family. A big country boy, Reese was born and raised on the farm, where several generations of his family have run cattle and sheep. His dad, Bill, is the county sheriff, while his mom, Shirley, is one of the best cooks I've ever met. The joy these people bring to my life is one of the main reasons I love spending time with them, and were it not for hunting, our paths would have never crossed.

The muleys in this region live amid deep cut banks and small cliffs, which can be good and bad for the bowhunter. The overall habitat consists of grassland, sage flats and badlands-type terrain. The approach is to spot the deer moving from feeding to bedding areas, then stalk in for a shot. Sometimes you can intercept the deer on the move, other times they are stalked in their beds.

The gumbo ridges of the badlands-type habitat makes for great spot-and-stalk mule deer hunting.

The year prior to this hunt, I was with Reese and we worked hard for six days. Each day I had multiple stalking opportunities, but couldn't close the deal. I learned a lot about the animals and the land on that hunt, as never in my life had I had so many close calls and not filled a tag.

On the first stalk of the first morning on that hunt, Reese and I spied a 180-inch 4x4. We watched him through the spotting scope, his heavy, white antlers glistening in the cool, crisp morning light. When the buck bedded tight against a small cut bank, we felt I could get close enough for a shot.

After nearly two hours I was within 50 yards of the buck, though I couldn't see him. I approached from above and behind him, atop a grassy flat, and the cut against which he bedded was higher than I'd expected.

Slipping off my boots and sliding on another pair of thick socks to somewhat protect my feet from the cacti thorns, I inched forward. My camera man, Bret Stuart, did the same.

At 20 yards from the ledge, Bret stayed back while I slowly slithered forward. Finally, six yards from the edge, I could see the tines of the buck's rack. Arrow nocked, I slowly came to my knees and reached full-draw. Inching toward the edge, I was now three yards from the buck, and realized at that point, getting a shot was going to be impossible. It would have been easier to reach out and slap his rack with my hand than it would have been to get a shot with my bow. When I let the bow down, the buck spooked and rambled off.

Due to the steep cut banks, stalking within close range of a bedded muley is fairly simple–getting a clear shot is another story.

I learned a valuable lesson on that stalk, namely that no matter how good your stalking skills may be, it doesn't mean you are going to get a shot. But, I'm a slow learner sometimes and later that day made the same mistake on a buck I closed to within eight yards of. The next day I moved to within five yards of another bedded buck, and couldn't get a shot. Though getting so close on these stalks was a rush, all I was doing was educating the deer.

Finally, on the last evening of that first hunt, Reese spotted a buck with a herd of does. The deer were on the move, and I was able to use the broken terrain to move ahead of them. When they came walking out from behind a gumbo mound, the 22 yard shot was simple and the 4-point buck didn't go far before expiring.

As in all hunting, every stalk I made with Reese was a learning experience, and there are far too many to relive in these pages. Bottom line, I was learning and was becoming a better bowhunter with each mistake I made. When it comes to hunting, there's no substitute for practical experience, and the only way to acquire that is by spending time in the field, stalking game.

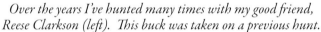

Over the years I've hunted many times with my good friend, Reese Clarkson (left). This buck was taken on a previous hunt.

Following my missed shot at the first buck on this hunt, we had multiple stalks over the next few days, but nothing I could capitalize on. Then, on Halloween morning, we caught a break.

Though the rut was on, Reese spotted a lone buck from well over a mile away. We watched as the buck moved up a gumbo ridge and laid down tight against a cut bank. We'd seen this scenario played-out dozens of times and by now I was getting used to passing such opportunities. Then we found a recessed cut in the terrain behind the buck.

"See what you can do if you slip in above him," Reese encouraged. "If you don't have a shot from there, try dropping below him, into that little dip and see if that might give you a shot."

With those words I was off. That night had been cold, below zero, which explained why the buck sought some early morning relief in the sun. When Bret and I left the truck, it had warmed up to 9°.

Wasting no time, Bret and I circled behind the buck. We wanted to get on him quick, before he warmed-up and moved off. We'd actually seen this buck the day before, and he was chasing does and sparring with two other bucks, so we knew his testosterone was running high. The last 75 yards of the stalk, however, moved tediously slow.

A slight breeze now whisked across our faces and the frozen, crunchy ground slowed our progress. With the wind, temperatures plummeted to below zero and my face grew numb; I knew my hands would soon follow.

At 30 yards from the buck I finally caught sight of the tops of his tines and realized there was no getting a shot from above. Backtracking and slipping down into the depression behind the bedded buck, the shot was going to have to come from here or not at all.

As I made my move, Bret got settled above and behind me. Looking through the tiny eyepiece of a 35-pound camera makes for tough walking, and we didn't want to spook the deer. Closing the distance on the buck, I glanced back at Bret for confirmation all was good. When I saw Bret curled-up, camera setting on the ground, I figured the buck had busted us.

I was wearing a wireless microphone, so whispered to Bret if the buck was gone. He motioned "No." Camera men are wired to hear me, but I can't hear them. This makes communicating with them difficult at times. Bret then pointed to his right hand, as he tried warming it up. Due to the tiny buttons on the camera, and Bret's big paws, he always ran a camera with his gloves off. We'd been in the cold elements for nearly 30 minutes now, and Bret's hands were in extreme pain.

After a few minutes Bret gave me the nod, and the hunt was back on. The gumbo dirt was frozen, making for solid footing with each step I took. When I crested a small berm, I could see the buck's rack. He was still bedded in the same place, facing straight away.

Hitting the back of his head with the rangefinder, I got 17 yards. The buck was laying with his chest slightly above his hind-end, giving me the perfect angle. He was tipped somewhat on his right side, favoring the hill, which exposed his body nicely.

Putting the 20 yard pin behind the last rib, just over his hind quarter, I vividly recall not being able to feel the kisser button in the corner of my mouth. My face and lips were so cold, I couldn't feel a thing. Searching for the kisser with my tongue, I confirmed it was in the right spot, and let the arrow fly.

My Bowtech Tribute speedily delivered the arrow to the exact hair I was aiming at. The 100 grain broadhead hit with a solid whack, lodging into the brisket of the sleeping big buck. The vanes on my Gold Tip Pro 400 arrow were barely visible as the buck shot to his feet and ambled over the ridge.

The Halloween buck arrowed at 17 yards. It's spot-and-stalk action on bucks like this that keep bringing me back to this corner of South Dakota.

Why I love mule deer hunting in South Dakota.

Reese had been watching from afar, and gave me the high-sign when the buck collapsed. I'd lost sight of the deer, but Reese had his eyes on him the whole way.

When I went back to give Bret a congratulatory hug, he was in immense pain. He'd lost all feeling in his right hand and was seconds away from not being able to capture the action on film. I lived for several years in Alaska's Arctic, where dealing with subzero temperatures was a routine occurrence. Frostbite is a very painful ordeal, and Bret's bare hands on the cold, metal camera, caused some nerve damage. For more than six months Bret's hand was numb and tingling before finally recovering from that hunt. That's the price camera men pay to get the job done and deliver award-winning TV shows. They are the true unsung heros of outdoor television, no question.

Approaching the downed buck, I knew he'd be pushing the 29-inch spread Reese had estimated. Over the years I've taken some good bucks with Clarkson, but this was one of the biggest bodied muleys I'd ever tagged, with bow or rifle. The fact he'd broken one of his tines, didn't matter, as this was all about the stalk on a wide-racked, wise old buck.

The rewards of a hard-earned hunt were realized, and on journeys like this, TV camera's in-tow, there's no greater thrill than getting the job done right. With incredible footage, a happy guide and the weight of the world off my shoulders, we celebrated Halloween that night at Bill and Shirley's house. Shirley's famous Navajo tacos keep bringing me back to this wonderful place, but as long as Reese keeps thinking it's his big mule deer bucks, that's fine with me.

Chapter 3:

Consolation Blacktail

I've been fortunate to hunt many species of big game around the world. Of all that I've pursued throughout North America, I feel trophy Columbia blacktail deer are the toughest to consistently attain. On this hunt I was close to a monster buck, but never saw him. Still, the buck I ended up with keeps me smiling every time I look at him on my den wall.

"You should get out here right away, the buck you're after just chased a doe across the lower end of the property," urged the voice of the landowner on the other end of the phone line. I'd not hunted private, lowland habitat for blacktails much at all, and was still learning their behavior in this micro-habitat.

Eager to set eyes on this buck, I grabbed my bow, hopped in the truck and headed to the southern reaches of Eugene, Oregon. The 45 minute drive from my home in the Cascade foothills went slow, as I knew the big buck would likely be gone by the time I got there.

"He laid down right over there, right next to a doe, for nearly 30 minutes," the landowner piped, before I could even get out of my truck. "I wasn't 40 yards from him! He's a giant buck!"

What's giant to some people might be small to others, so when I quizzed the landowner about how big giant was, he let me know. I'd met the landowner a few months prior, and knew he was a very successful mule deer hunter–the giant racks he had on his wall cemented the fact he knew what he was talking about. "Our family has lived here over 30 years," he shared, "and this is the biggest buck I've ever seen. He'll go at least 25-inches wide, and has multiple points on each side of his rack... but the cool thing, he has two matching 9-inch drop tines on each side. He's incredible!"

Over the years there have been some smasher blacktails taken from the south hills bordering Eugene. It's a private land deal, for sure, but just like big bucks across the nation–be they whitetails or muleys–some of the biggest of the big bucks live near populated areas. Here, the deer have year-round, easy living with plenty of food and few predators.

For the remainder of the afternoon I sat on the lower end of the property, looking for the buck. Though I saw plenty of deer, the double drop tine buck never showed.

The following morning found me in the same spot, well ahead of daylight. I sat, quietly, this time in a treestand. The slight breeze was perfect and the heavy November rain that had just moved through gave the forest a calming aura. The property consisted of a hefty stand of 50-year old Douglas firs that had been thinned out and was surrounded by thick brush, mainly ferns and vine maple. The deer would bed in the brushy fringes then come to feed on the green grasses and clover growing under the sparse canopy of fir trees.

My intent was to catch the does out feeding, hoping the rutting buck would follow. It was the middle of November, prime time for Oregon's late archery blacktail season. This is a time when many good bucks are taken, while other tags go unfilled by hunters set on taking a monster buck or nothing.

Though I'd not seen the double drop tine buck, I'd told myself it was him or nothing. I'd soon eat those words.

About noon on that second day, I had to head home to get some work done. When I arrived, there was a message awaiting me on the answering machine (we didn't have cell phones then). "Scott, he's back, right where I saw him yesterday," the landowner shared. "You'd better get back here, he's laying right under your stand!"

So, I headed right back out there. Of course, the buck was gone, and didn't show himself again that evening.

The next morning found me in the same place, and though does were moving, I didn't see any sign of the big buck. Some smaller bucks were milling around, acting rutty, but no good bucks showed.

I tried rattling but nothing responded except a couple small spikes and forked-horns. I tried some doe bleats from time to time, and did

As within most blacktail habitats, the deer in this area were bedding in thick cover, then coming to feed along open edges just before dark.

draw in some does, but no bucks were following. I'd dedicated myself to sitting in the stand the whole day, right up until dark.

With less than 30 minutes of hunting light left, movement of a doe caught my attention in the draw below. She was 200 yards away, moving through thick vine maple, headed toward a sword fern patch. I could see glimpses of a mature buck following her, but couldn't make out what he was.

In late season blacktail hunts, as long as does are in the area, there's a chance a giant buck can show up at any moment.

As she picked her way through the ferns, the buck followed, heading straight for me. Then, about 100 yards out, she turned and began feeding up the draw. I tried a series of doe bleats and buck grunts but neither deer so much as looked my way.

Daylight was burning and it was obvious the deer weren't going to come my way. I looked at the buck through my binos' and though he wasn't the double drop tine buck, I knew he was one I had to try for. His rack was fairly massive and tall, with some nontypical points here and there.

The second the deer moved out of sight I hopped from the tree, ducked behind the ridge and ran up the hill. Covering about 200 yards, my intent was to intercept the deer as they continued up the hill.

Stealthing over the crown of the ridge, I searched hard for the doe and buck. Nothing. Creeping closer to the deer trail in the bottom, still I failed to find them. Situating myself behind a rotten stump, I sat, hoping to catch sight of something. Staring through my binoculars, I picked apart every piece of brush in front of me. I could clearly see down into the draw, and across the other side, but nothing.

Reaching for the doe bleat, I froze. Right in front of me–inside 40 yards–the doe popped out from behind a tiny curtain of young cedar trees. Right behind her came the buck. The second they moved behind another tree, I anchored, trying to calm my nerves for the shot.

The buck stopped, barely 30 yards away. All I could see was his head; his lips curling, nose wet, trying to take in the message the doe's hormones were sending. Then he rub-urinated all over his tarsal glands. He was rutting hard, which gave me the break I needed.

As the doe moved forward, the buck followed. It was obvious the buck wasn't the monster the landowner had been seeing, the one I'd earlier dedicated myself to shooting. But the deer I held in my sights was big, an obvious record book blacktail and the biggest buck I'd ever pointed an arrow at.

When the buck drifted into the open and paused, I let the arrow fly. My adrenaline level was high, making it tough to remain steady. Still, the shot felt good, and I immediately began trembling with excitement. The buck jumped and bolted, but quickly slowed to a quivering walk. The arrow had passed clean through, and was sticking out of the ground on the other side of where the buck stood. The white fletches were covered in blood.

I did hit the buck a bit farther back than I'd hoped, and when he continued stumbling out of sight, over the far ridge, my heart sank. Still, as slow as he was moving, and the fact he was heading downhill, I felt confident he wouldn't go much further.

It's amazing how tough big game animals can be. Admittedly, it wasn't the best shot, but that's bowhunting. Giving the buck plenty of time, I followed-up with a flashlight. The blood was good, but not the bright red, bubbly blood I'd hoped for. It was liver blood, and though I knew it was a lethal shot, I had to give the buck time. The last thing I wanted to do was push him from the property, on to a neighbor's place, and have to go through the ordeal of explaining my predicament to a stranger. This private land hunting was becoming stressful.

The next morning I was back in the woods, picking up the blood trail where I'd left off. I didn't go another 50 yards, and there was my buck. In all, he went about 175 yards–further than I'd hoped, but not as bad as it could have been.

Wrapping my fingers around the massive rack, this was the first time I got to see how big he really was. Sporting six tines on each side, he was

*Though not the buck I was after, I couldn't pass
on this 6x6, record class blacktail.*

the largest buck I'd arrowed up to that point in my life. I couldn't have been happier as I loaded the deer into the truck and headed for home.

Later that day, the landowner called, "The double drop tine buck is back!" Sadly, I never did lay eyes on that colossal deer. I hunted him for two more seasons and no one, not even the landowner, ever saw him again. I'm confident that buck died of old age, for had a hunter taken him, word would have spread fast in the blacktail community.

I was elated with the great buck I'd taken, as he was a striking animal to behold even though he was a consolation to the monster that roamed the region. The moment I raised my bow on that buck, I thought to myself, "Pass this buck and you'll never forgive yourself." I made the right choice.

BOWHUNTING THE WEST & BEYOND

Chapter 4:

3 Tags, 3 Days, 3 Speedgoats!

Spot-and-stalk pronghorn hunting is one of bowhunting's greatest challenges. So, when three hunters take to the field, and fill three tags in three days, you know it must be a special place.

Less than 10 minutes into the hunt, good friend Clay White, was in the middle of his first pronghorn stalk. He didn't think the action would start so fast, but soon learned this would be the norm.

Unfortunately, after nearly and hour of stalking, the buck busted Clay. The good part, a few minutes later Clay was on another stalk. Then another. By mid-morning Clay had made four good stalks, none of which came together.

It was late August and we were back with Reese Clarkson in South Dakota. I'd hunted muleys with Reese in the past, and that's when I became aware of the incredible number of pronghorns running around his land. Not to mention, the habitat these antelope call home seems to have been custom-made for the bowhunter.

Though sitting at a waterhole and shooting a buck from a ground blind was a high percentage proposition, we wanted to use the land and our hunting skills to try and close the deal on foot. Clay, myself and mutual friend, C.J. Davis, all held tags, and all three of us committed to spotting and stalking our antelope. The toughest part, we wanted to catch all the action on film for BowTech's Western Adventures TV show I was hosting at the time.

Shortly after noon on the first day, Clay and Reese headed across a sage-covered draw, intent on trying to decoy a trio of bucks in the distance. When Reese popped-up the decoy about 200 yards from the bachelor group of bucks, all three lifted their heads and started moving toward the hunters. It wasn't a fast, all-out run like you'd expect, but they were getting closer.

Minutes passed and the hunters stayed put, decoy still in position. Now the bucks were within 100 yards. Occasionally one buck would stop, make a scrape, then move forward. At one point two of the bucks started sparring, then they quit and kept walking toward the decoy.

When they were 50 yards out–all three bucks still coming closer– Clay knew it was going to happen. The biggest of the bucks paused to rub the black scent glands of his face on a stiff branch of sage brush, and Clay ranged him at 30 yards. When the buck was done rubbing, he turned broadside, staring at the decoy.

Reese slowly slid the decoy forward, giving Clay, who was already at full-draw, the clearance he needed to shoot. At that distance, the arrow zipped through the speedgoat and he took off on an all-out sprint. The buck went over a small rise and quickly piled-up in a cloud of dust. One tag was filled and Clay couldn't have been happier.

Clay White got the hunt off to a great start with this gorgeous pronghorn taken by way of spot-and-stalk.

That afternoon, C.J. got on two stalks, one of which I'll never forget. Reese had spotted a big buck bedded down with a harem of eight does. They were in the wide-open, and with too many eyes and not enough cover to put on a stalk, Reese and C.J. took the decoy and snuck around the bottom edge of a gumbo ridge.

No sooner had Reese slid the head of the decoy in sight of the herd, and the buck sprang to his feet. Ears alert, nostrils flared, the buck wasted no time. Immediately he reached top speed, covering the 125 yards in a few short seconds.

C.J. quickly came to full-draw, but when the buck screeched to a halt at barely 10-yards, there was no shot. The buck came in so fast, it didn't give Reese enough time to get the decoy out from behind the gumbo knob, and C.J. was stuck behind it. The instant C.J. lifted his bow, trying to clear the gumbo hill, the buck snorted and took off.

That night at the dinner table, the room was a buzz with exciting stories from the day. What we would give to have another repeat performance.

By mid-morning of the second day, C.J. would commence on multiple stalks, but either too many eyes or a lack of interest in the decoy would botch any shot opportunities. C.J. was close on several attempts, and we all knew his persistence would pay dividends.

Hunting behind decoys is one of the most exciting ways to go about arrowing a pronghorn.

C.J. Davis makes his living through outdoor marketing. He intimately knows the hunting business and bowhunting. This is the second record book pronghorn he's taken while hunting with me.

Later that afternoon a lone buck was spotted roaming a big sage brush flat. Ducking into the bottom of a little ravine, Reese's ace guide, Scott Koan, felt he could get C.J. close enough for a shot. This is where having someone along who knows the detailed contours of the land is invaluable. From where we all sat, watching that buck, it seemed there was no prayer of getting close enough for a shot.

Thirty minutes later, Scott and C.J. were within 50 yards of the buck, which was now bedded. Unable to get a shot, C.J. inched forward ever so cautiously. After only a few seconds the buck got up, stretched and gave C.J. the perfect shot opportunity. At just over 40 yards, the shot was perfect. Over the years I've shot a lot with C.J., and he's one of the best shooters, under pressure, that I've been around.

Just like that, two days, two tags filled. It was seeming that our six day trip was going to end early. Then again, this is bowhunting and there are never any guarantees.

The next morning it was my turn. Reese, Scott Koan and I, along with camera man, Bret Stuart, headed out. Less than five minutes into the hunt, Scott spotted two good bucks with a herd of does. Quickly, we dropped out of sight, into the bottom of a draw, popped up the decoy and continued forward.

By the time we reached the point where the pronghorns could see us, they were over 150-yards away. Still, Koan felt the decoy would work, as the bucks were aggressively chasing does.

It took them a few minutes but when the biggest buck finally caught glimpse of our decoy amid some tall sage brush, he tore up the turf, heading straight for us. To reach us, the buck had to drop down in a draw, meaning we'd lose sight of him for about 50 yards.

Taking the line of sight we'd last seen the buck traveling, both Scott and I guessed what trail the buck would appear on. If it worked, great, if not, whatever happened was going to do so at close range.

Figuring the buck was close, I anchored my BowTech Tribute and held steady. Nothing. After more than a minute, I let down, and still there was no sign of the buck. "He's got to be down there," Scott whispered. "There's no way for him to get out of that draw without us seeing him."

Then, to our right, the big buck magically appeared, less than 10 yards away! The angle was so severe, there was no prayer of getting a shot. The buck came in facing the decoy, not from the side as we'd hoped. That meant we were the only things he could really see, rather than the decoy. As soon as he made us, he was gone.

I was amazed how close the buck had come. "We've had them come in so close to this young buck decoy, they've actually brushed up against it," Scott smiled, folding up the decoy as we walked back to the rig.

When the pronghorn rut is on, anything can happen.

By mid-afternoon I had several stalks behind me and was learning with each mistake made along the way. The best part of this hunt was the sheer number of stalks we got each day. There was never more than two minutes during our three days of hunting where we weren't either watching antelope, planning a stalk or putting on a stalk. Plain and simple, it was the best bowhunting experience I'd ever had for these great ghosts of the prairie. We were receiving years of education on a daily basis.

Early that evening we found a buck bedded all alone in some sage brush. The good part, the sage in which he laid was tall enough to offer enough cover for a stalk. The bad part, he'd have to be approached from head-on. Considering the keen eyesight of these ungulates, I gave this stalk a very low chance of actually working. But, it was a dandy buck, and you never know unless you try.

Scott got me lined-out on an ideal path of travel. From there, he turned Bret, my camera man, and I loose. We covered ground quickly for the first couple hundred yards, then the dry, crunchy ground slowed our progress. Daytime winds were dying down and with the ground so noisy, and the fact the buck was facing us, the odds of success seemed to rapidly deteriorate.

Nonetheless, we pushed on. Not until we got within 60 yards of the buck did Bret and I finally see him for the first time. He was still bedded in the same spot, which was good for us. Being this close yet knowing we'd have to get much closer, we removed our shoes. Walking in sock-feet amid cactus-laden land is not the brightest move, but it's helped me close the deal on many early season archery hunts for pronghorn, mule deer, elk and other prized game around the world.

At 40 yards, Bret decided to stay back and film the stalk from there. All we could see was the buck's horns and the top of his black head, which meant I had to get closer, much closer.

When I reached 30 yards I felt there was no chance of getting an arrow into this buck. The angle at which he was bedded, and given the amount of brush between us, I simply didn't feel it could be done.

By now, the slow, tedious, stalk had been underway for nearly two hours. Inch by painful inch I moved forward. I'd been belly-crawling for the last 20 yards, and the feeling of thorns piercing my body was almost more than I could take.

When crawling along the desert floor like this, it's not the fresh green cacti that gives you fits, it's the dead brown ones. Once the cacti die, the plant turns brown, blending in perfectly with the ground. But the cacti spines are still needle-sharp. These are the ones you devote hours to digging out of your body when the hunt comes to a close.

With nerves on end, I knew I was getting close, too close. At 22 yards I ranged the buck and knew it was now or never. The only thing that allowed me to get so close was a thick stub of sage brush that covered the buck's left eye. Every time I moved forward, I made certain that branch was covering the buck's eye. That's one reason I had to crawl through so many cacti, because my line of travel was being determined for me.

The buck was still laying down with his head slightly quartering to me. At this point I knew I had to take the shot. Slowly, I rose to my knees. At the same time, I smoothly brought the Tribute to full-draw and shifted my body to the right, which put the sage branch about even with the end of the buck's nose, exposing his neck and upper chest. Now I could see the entire left side of his face, and was dumbfounded when the buck didn't bolt.

Wasting no time, I held my 20 yard pin high on the buck's bottom throat patch. The low-profile broadhead and Gold Tip arrow were driven out of sight, through the buck's entire body cavity and out the hind end, near the base of his tail.

The buck sprang to his feet and ran in the direction he was facing, straight at me. When I stood, the buck saw me and veered to the side, missing me by about 10 yards. But he continued on his death-run, brushing by Bret at only a few yards. With each stride, blood poured from the entry wound. The buck didn't make it 50 yards before piling-up in a small, grassy draw a few steps from where Bret stood.

It was one of the most gratifying stalks of my life and I was fired-up! I was feeling pretty good about myself, and the adrenaline that coursed through my veins only added to the sheer joy of the hunt.

We met up with Scott, Reese and the gang. That's when Scott opened his mouth. "Hey, look at this! Here's why you were able to get so close."

We gathered around the buck, looking at his battle-scarred face. The old buck had been in a recent fight and his face showed it. His left eye had been gouged out. He was totally blind in his left eye.

"Way to go Haugen," the prodding began. "You just shot a crippled buck!"

"No wonder you got so close, this buck was blind!"

A lengthy stalk on this bedded pronghorn, then connecting on a 22 yard frontal shot, made for one of my most memorable bowhunting moments, ever.

"So, how do you feel about shooting a buck that just got beat-up and blinded?

Now, years later, I'm still not living that one down. Nonetheless, it was a thrilling stalk on a record book buck and I couldn't have been happier.

Nine months after that hunt, I finally got the last of the infected cacti spines out of my knee. Every day for nine months I felt the pain of that spine, a vivid reminder of not only that stalk, but of the best three days of pronghorn hunting I've ever experienced.

Chapter 5:

The Toughest Bear of All

When pursued in the rugged, jungle-like Coast Range of northern California, chasing a pack of hounds after bears is one of the most grueling hunts the West has to offer. Throw in a driving rain, 9 hours without food or water and mauled dogs, and the journey reaches a whole new level.

"Turn 'em loose right here," instructed Kenny Gavin, longtime houndsman from the northwest corner of California. "There's a road in the bottom of the canyon and another on the opposite ridge, so we should be okay."

It was barely light enough to see across the rugged mountains, but only minutes into the hunt, the dogs had already caught scent of a bear. A heavy mist fell, keeping the bear's scent on the ground and after looking at the tracks of where the bruin crossed the road, Kenny guessed it to be a good boar. Quickly, Kenny and I unleashed the dogs from atop their box and the chase was on.

Pulling the truck to the side of the logging road, we listened. Ten minutes later we could still hear the hounds chasing the bear in the lower part of the canyon. A good 500 yards from where we sat, by the sound of the hounds bawling, Kenny could tell when the bear was on the move or bayed-up, on the ground.

Then the tone of the hounds changed. "That's it, he's treed!" barked Kenny. "Grab your bow, let's go get that bear, then while your skinning it I can come back up for the truck and meet you in the bottom."

The whole thing seemed pretty straight forward; too good to be true. Then again, this wasn't my first time hunting bears with hounds. In fact, I'd been on several hound hunts over the years and can never get enough of them. However, every time I embark upon such a hunt in the deep, rugged canyons of the Coast Range, I usually vow never to return. For some reason, I keep coming back.

When my home state of Oregon banned the use of hounds for bear and cougar hunting, it greatly impacted the dynamics of big game populations throughout the state. Both bear and cougar are a detriment to deer, elk, even some bighorn sheep populations. Hunting these predators with hounds is the most efficient way to keep their numbers in-check.

In 2009, while writing an article for a national magazine, I interviewed a biologist in the northeast corner of Oregon who claimed bears were killing over 70% of the elk calves in one of the game management units. With record bear and cougar populations occurring statewide, Oregon has seen a dramatic decline in some of it's blacktail, mule deer and elk herds. Other predators, like bobcats, coyotes and wolves are also impacting ungulate populations throughout the West.

Hound hunting is one of the most sound tools of black bear management there is. Once treed, animals can be selectively taken or set free. It's also the most effective way to find these big predators who live amid some of the country's most dense habitat, making them tough to hunt and consistently take through other hunting methods.

When the state of Oregon, and others in the West, banned hunting with hounds, it was a grave mistake. It marked a pivotal time in wildlife management, for now these elusive predators were being managed by the public's emotions–many of whom were non-hunters, nor trained biologists.

Not only are valuable deer and elk being killed by bears and cougars, but the bears are killing countless trees in states like California and Washington. The bears strip the bark and eat the cambium layer of young trees, whereby killing them. As if losing hundreds of thousands of dollars which would eventually be brought in to the economy through tag sales, excise taxes and more while hunting big game, isn't enough, now timber companies are losing literally millions of dollars in timber each year. States who have banned hunting with hounds need to rectify it fast, before it's too late.

Grabbing my bow, I followed Kenny, headlong into the wet brush. By now the rain had picked up. It wasn't just a drizzle, this was the type of rain the Pacific Northwest is infamous for and it was supposed to get worse as the day went on.

Crossing a knee-deep creek, getting wet didn't matter, for even the best of raingear wasn't going to keep us dry from the storm that was about to hit. Within 20 minutes we were under the tree, the pack of hounds bawling so intensely, Kenny and I couldn't hear one another talk.

One of hunting's great thrills, and most demanding hunts, is following a pack of fired-up hounds through the rugged Coast Range.

While Kenny grabbed the hounds and tied them off to some small trees on the uphill side of the bear, I searched for a window through which to thread an arrow. The bear was only about 40 feet up in the tree, but he laid flat across a giant limb, which blocked his vitals. No matter where I moved, there was simply no shot.

"Just wait, he'll move," Kenny encouraged.

About then the bear moved, alright. He stood up, turned around on the limb and started backing down the tree so fast, I couldn't hold steady on him. I'm always amazed at how fast bears can back out of a tree when they want to.

Anchored at full-draw, all I needed was a small window of opportunity. As the bear backed down, wrapping himself around the tree, I kept moving, trying to get a shot. Just before he hit the ground, he was no more than three feet from me, but it all happened so fast, I couldn't shoot.

Immediately Kenny cut the dogs loose and the chase was on, once again. This time the bear headed straight up the canyon and we were committed to following, on foot.

Running through thick, wet brush, over big, fallen timber and spending much time face-first on the ground, I was drenched more from sweat than the cold rain which was now making it very difficult to hear the hounds barking. Still, we pushed on.

Two hours and I don't know how many miles later of running, up, down and across that canyon and it's many ridges, the bear finally treed. Due to the thick brush and near vertical terrain the bear entered, it took Kenny and I another hour to reach the tree.

Again, Kenny tethered the dogs while I searched for a shooting window. Less than 20 yards away, this time the bear's vitals were perfectly exposed. We knew, given the angle, it was going to be a one-lung shot, which meant either the bear would stay in the tree or get out as fast as he could after the shot, and likely run a fair distance.

As soon as the arrow found it's mark, the bear was coming down the tree. Kenny and I ran to the base of the tree, hollering, trying to force the bear back up, but the brute had already made up his mind to come down. When the bear hit the ground, two feet from where I stood, he was headed on an all-out sprint, crashing through the brush, straight downhill. I was relieved when he headed away, not straight for me.

Our intent was to give the bear about 20 minutes, then turn the dogs loose on the blood trail. But the moment the bear hit the ground, one of the dogs broke free. Before we could grab him, the hound was off, tight on the bear's tail.

Grabbing the other hounds, Kenny kept them on their leashes and headed after the bear. The brush quickly grew thick, and the powerful pack of relentless hounds ripped the tethers from Kenny's hands. We knew we had to move fast or the dogs could be killed by the enraged, injured bear.

We didn't go 50 yards and found two of the dogs hanging from a log. The dog's leashes had gotten tangled with one another and when they tried running on opposite sides of a log which hung 10-feet off the ground, over an embankment, they got caught on the end of it. Had we not gotten to them when we did, they would have strangled themselves. Fortunately, as we cut the dogs loose, they wasted no time getting back on the trail.

A pack of hounds trailing a bear trail is something that has to be experienced in order to be fully understood and appreciated. The unrelenting nature of the hounds and how they work together is unlike any form of hunting I know. They risk life and limb for the sake of the hunt.

We hadn't gone 75 yards when we found our bear, bayed-up, swatting at dogs as they flung themselves at him. It was obvious the bear was hurting from the shot, and the smell of blood only enraged the already over-aggressive hounds.

The swarming pack of six dogs kept me from getting another arrow into the bear, and though Kenny had his .30-30 lever action along for backup, there was no way he could get a shot, either. Then the bear rolled over on his side and disappeared into a tall patch of sword ferns, tumbling over a small embankment.

When we popped over the edge, the bear had one of the dogs in his jaws, shaking him like a rag doll by the stomach. Kenny dove down the embankment and with the butt of his rifle, smashed it

Following a quick clean-up, I grabbed a couple dogs and gathered around the bear for some photos. This was one of the most grueling hunts of my life.

across the bear's skull. The dogs were all over the bear and Kenny didn't want to risk injuring one with with a stray bullet, so resorted to whacking the bear with the butt of his trusty .30-30. On the third blow to the head, the gun stock broke. Then, finally, the ordeal was over. The hunt had ended.

Examining the hounds, a couple had minor bite and claw marks. The one being shaken by the bear carried deep puncture wounds in his abdomen, and we knew we needed to get him to a vet, soon. Another dog had an open gash across his stomach, and Kenny shoved his intestines back inside.

It had been pouring rain for over three hours now, and was coming down so hard, Kenny and I had to shout at the top of our lungs to even hear one another. Quickly, we devised a plan.

We were only a few hundred yards from the creek bottom, the same creek we'd crossed at the start of the hunt. The plan was for me to carry the most severely injured dog back to the truck, two miles up the gorge, keeping his internal organs intact. I'd lead the other injured dog as best I could.

Kenny would take the four remaining dogs and the bear about four miles down the creek, where I'd meet him with the truck. The idea was for Kenny to float the bear downstream, with the rest of the pack following him.

Rather than walk the uneven, rocky shoreline of the creek bottom, I headed through the forest toward where we originally crossed the stream. By the time I reached water's edge, two, maybe three miles separated Kenny and I. What I now faced, I couldn't believe. Instead of a creek, I was staring at a raging river.

Muddy and flowing three-feet higher than what it was four hours prior, I barely recognized the raging stream. Frantically searching for a place to cross, I finally found a section that was only chest-deep.

With the aid of a walking staff, I stumbled across the creek and set my bow and pack on the other side. The water was so high, I had to carry them above my head with one hand, bracing myself with the staff in the other.

Grabbing the severely injured dog, I tossed him over my shoulders, around my neck, and headed across. To this day, how I made it across that boulder-strewn stream without falling is beyond me, but we did it. Only a few times in the ordeal did I have to poke protruding intestines back into the dog's gut cavity.

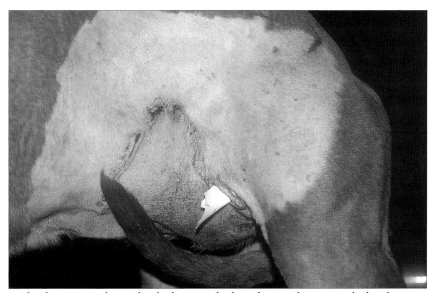

After being ripped open by the bear, and white drain tube removed, this dog was sewn up and back in the woods in less than a month.

Going back across for the dog on the leash, there was no way to get him to swim the rampaging stream. I tried carrying him, but the dog would have nothing of it. This dog was much more lively than the other injured dog which lay on the opposite bank.

After trying everything I could think of to get that second dog across, his resistance was growing more aggressive. Then he broke free from my grasp and took off back downstream, in Kenny's direction. I had no choice but to let him go.

Loading up the other dog, it would take me another hour of driving to reach the point where I was to meet Kenny. I was only imagining what he was going through.

When I got to our meeting spot, there was no sign of Kenny or the dogs. Hiking upstream, I searched and hollered, but saw nor heard a thing. Then a dog popped into view, followed by another. I grabbed them, loaded them in the dog box and drove up and down the road, looking for more dogs and Kenny.

The injured dog I couldn't get to cross the creek was staggering down the road, and I got him loaded. Going back to the designated meeting spot, this time I hiked about a half-mile up the stream before I found Kenny.

He was soaking wet, and without the bear. With a rope around the bear's neck, Kenny tried floating it downstream. Wet bears don't float.

When the 250-pound bruin got waterlogged, it gained immense weight and combined with the raging stream, it was all Kenny could do to hang on.

Working the bear through shallow riffles wasn't too bad, but when Kenny hit a deep, swirling pool, he got dragged down and pulled underwater. Battling the boiling water and erratic currents, it was all Kenny could do to free the rope from around his wrist and reach the surface. Swimming to shore, Kenny felt lucky to be alive.

Searching the banks of the stream, which was now more river-like than ever, Kenny spotted the bear, it's jet black hide almost glowing blue in the water. It took all our combined strength but we were able to pull the bear ashore, force the water from his hide, wrestle him onto the dog box and hit the road.

Nine hours had elapsed since we first set foot in the woods. Now it was dark.

Rushing the two injured dogs to the vet, one required immediate surgery, the others, a stiff dose of antibiotics. The following day, Kenny and I returned to the woods and found the other two dogs wandering the logging road.

Three weeks later the injured dogs were back in the woods, chasing bears. It's amazing how tough these dogs are and how deeply they yearn for the hunt. These hounds, like their masters, are a different breed from what many hunters know, and I'm always thrilled, and honored, to be a part of such hunts.

Chapter 6:

Valley of the Bulls

Once in a great while you find yourself in the middle of a hunt where, what unfolds dramatically surpasses your wildest expectations. You revel in these thrills, hoping they never end. This British Columbia elk hunt was one such adventure.

As the bush plane banked hard on it's final approach into base camp, my eyes strained to see any elk on the nearby hillsides. Off both wingtips it was easy spotting mountain goats as they grazed above treeline, their white winter coats a sharp contrast to the gray and green habitat they call home.

Giant moose were simple to spot in the valleys, their large, paddle-like antlers glistening in the mid-day sun. But no elk.

After touching down on the dirt runway and taxiing into camp, I was greeted by Larry and Lori Warren, owners of Tuchodi River Outfitters. "Did you see any critters?" Larry quizzed with a firm handshake. "Goat and moose, but no elk," I shared. "Don't worry, there's a few around," he smiled, reaching for my bags.

Though it was the allure of mountain goats and moose which initially drew me to this land, it was also late September and the elk rut was in full-swing. The Tuchodi River drainage is acclaimed to host what could be Canada's largest roaming herd of Rocky Mountain elk. I would soon discover why this accolade might ring true.

It was 1974 when Lori first set foot in this camp. Then, as a young lady, she worked her first job as camp cook. In 1983, Larry Warren made his way into camp for the first time, working as a guide.

In 1999, the Warrens, having long since been married, began managing the operation, and in 2005 bought it, outright. Today,

Tuchodi River Outfitters is known in big game circles as a premier destination for Stone sheep, mountain goat, moose and elk.

Over the course of the year, up to 20 guides, wranglers and cooks will make up the Tuchodi staff. With multiple camps and 150 head of horses to manage, not to mention the more than four million acres the Warrens have access to, this is not a simple operation to maintain. But they do it, and do it well.

Following a nice lunch, it didn't take long to unpack and get my bow tuned-in. I was shooting BowTech's new Admiral, the first bow of it's kind to leave the factory. I was especially thrilled with the prospects of being the first person to arrow an animal with this quiet, smooth-handling bow. Set at 71 pounds, it was launching my 355 grain Gold Tip arrow right at 300 feet per second.

"There are a lot of bulls hanging around camp this year," Larry shared, tipping his cowboy hat to the hills. "We'll just walk from here."

Fifty yards from the cabin I saw my first sign of elk. Fresh tracks and droppings covered the edge of the aspen forest. Larry shot me a smile.

In less than 15 minutes we'd made it to the the first little knoll without even breaking a sweat. "Try calling," Larry encouraged. Putting light pressure on the open-reed call, I let out a seductive cow sound that

The Tuchodi River Valley is one
of the most breathtaking places I've ever set foot in.

carried up the valley. One bull answered, followed by two other bulls bugling farther up the draw.

"They're not real fired-up yet," Larry whispered as he headed up the trail.

Where I come from, three bulls answering the first call is as fired-up as they get. But Larry didn't give them a second thought. He led us farther into the green timber, above the quaking aspens.

A short time later I let out another series of cow calls, these directed into a different drainage. Two bulls answered back. A couple estrus cow calls got five more bulls to respond. "They're starting to wake up a little now," Larry muttered as he pushed on.

Over the course of the next three hours, we'd hear more than 20 bulls bugle. Eight of these bulls would approach to within 40 yards, but lacing an arrow through the thick brush was next to impossible.

During that three hour flurry, there wasn't more than a couple minutes where a bugling bull could not be heard. As the timber grew dark, it was obvious the bulls were quickly dropping in elevation, toward their nightly feeding grounds.

"We won't push them," Larry encouraged. I was in no hurry for the hunt to end on the first evening, not with so many bulls in the area. If nothing else, the first afternoon of hunting proved to be a memorable scouting mission.

As we followed the elk down the ridgelines, it became clear to me where they were heading...straight into the grassy flats to feed, the same meadows base-camp was situated in. Sleeping that night was tough. In fact, sleep hardly came at all as the echos of bulls filled the air.

Gazing at the bright, shimmering stars in the crisp, Canadian night, the sounds, sights and smells made the magical moment so vivid, so alive. Soon, a crackling fire lured me back into the cabin. Nestling inside the sleeping bag, I was relieved to hear the sounds of bugles making their way through the cabin walls. It lasted all night long.

By 5:00 a.m. the camp was active. Wranglers prepared the horses. Cooks whipped-up breakfast and bagged lunches. Hunters readied themselves for a day afield. The morning responsibilities were carried-out with impressive efficiency.

Soon we were riding into the hills, the quiet strides of horses barely breaking the morning silence. Before we could even make it into the timber, bulls bugled all around us.

"We need to get ahead of them before they reach the thick timber," Larry urged. We rode past several elk, calling from horseback as we went. No question our sounds calmed the bulls, for they continued bugling at our every call.

Dismounting, Larry tied off the horses while I set up to call. No sooner had the cow sounds passed my lips when a bull bugled back. Then another. As the two bulls approached, so did a third, from downwind. The minute the big 6x6 busted us, the gig was up, and all three elk were swallowed by dark timber.

Hopping back in the saddle, we continued farther up the ridge. This time, when a bull responded to our calls, he was close. Real close. Sliding off the horses, Larry grabbed the reigns while I scrambled into position. Larry called while I knocked an arrow.

Within seconds two bulls came crashing in to the calls. Both were nice five points, but not what we were looking for.

*On several occasions multiple bulls came
to the call. This one was left to grow another year.*

By now it was late morning and the bugles of distant bulls were high in the hills. The wind was also kicking up.

"Let's head into the trees, eat lunch and take a snooze," Larry encouraged. "There's no use calling in these windy conditions. We'll wait and see what it does this afternoon."

Mesmerized by falling, golden aspen leaves and elegant clouds whisking over the towering granite peaks, the sounds of bugling bulls rang clear in my mind. Settling into a cozy bed of thick, green moss, sleep came quickly on a full-stomach.

By 3:00 p.m. the wind was subsiding. "Let's head to the east side of the ridge, there's gotta be some elk up and feeding in the shaded draws," Larry suggested.

Twenty minutes later we were in calling position and a lone bull let out an impressive bugle in response to a cow mew. As I moved his direction, not anticipating his coming my way in such a rush, I was startled when the bull barked, whirled and crashed off through the brush. He'd covered more than 100 yards in a hurry, and I simply blew it by trying to get too close.

"No worry, I bet we can find another one," Larry winked.

A few minutes later a locator bugle got another bull to answer. This bull, too, came to the call, but winded us before I could let an arrow fly. He was a dandy 6x6 I would have loved tagging, but he outsmarted us.

Reaching the edge of an old burn, the habitat reeked of elk. Letting out a single cow call, five bulls responded. "They seem to be talking a bit this afternoon," said Larry, pulling a long straw of yellow grass from his teeth.

Given the wind, our only hope was to try and get ahead of the most distant bull, then resume calling. It wasn't easy, as open terrain and steep hillsides meant we would be exposed, but it was our only option.

Making it to our designated landmark we felt we were in good position to drop into the treeline, work the wind and start calling. Just as we got to where we wanted, another bull barked and scampered off. Every bull on that hillside immediately shut down.

Hiking back to the horses, it was getting late. With only enough time to try one more setup, we dropped into a wooded canyon. An excited cow call got four immediate replies, followed by a string of other bugles. In all, 12 bulls could be heard from that one spot. It was one of the most incredible moments of my hunting career.

With time running out, we moved into position, targeting the closest bull. Larry stayed 30 yards back, intermittently cow calling. I moved into the throat of a small ravine which offered multiple, though very tight, shooting lanes.

At my first calf sound, the bull rumbled back, no more than 50 yards distant. Crashing brush left no question as to what was unfolding. Arrow knocked, I waited. Again the bull bugled, followed by another bull to the left of him. Both bulls were coming hard.

As the duo trotted closer, I could hear their massive, heavy chest cavities taking in air. Glunks and bugles ensued, then the first bull materialized in front of me. He slipped by so quickly, I didn't have a shot. I didn't want to call and stop him as I'd not yet seen the second bull, and he could have been bigger.

As the first bull moved behind me, the second bull finally emerged from the brush. A definite shooter, his heavy rack was clearly evident in the tangled underbrush. I let out a quick cow call to stop him. It worked, and as he bugled, so did a third bull which was also barreling down the draw. The first bull that ran past also bugled, while outrageously thrashing a tree less than 40 yards behind me.

Getting a shot opportunity is all but guaranteed when hunting the Tuchodi River. I stopped my bull with the Mini Mouth, an open-reed call that can be clinched in the teeth and blown as needed.

Focused on the second bull, he, too was slipping by, headed towards Larry's calls. Again, no shot through the brush. Still at full-draw, I swung on bull number three.

I could see the bull's rack in the trees, and that he had stopped. Letting out a subtle sound with a Mini Mouth elk call—an open-reed call you can hold in your teeth and operate— he answered and edged forward. The second bull did a 180 and was coming back.

With no time to waste, for fear one of the three bulls would wind me, I swung back on bull number two. Tracking his massive body through the tangle of branches, I held my 30-yard pin tight behind his shoulder. Worried I'd not be able to get a shot, I moved the bow ahead of him, found a small opening in the brush and waited for the bull to walk into it.

As he walked forward I let out a sharp call on the Mini Mouth. The second he stopped, I shifted my sight pin into an ever-narrowing gap. Restricted by brush, vines, limbs and tree trunks, I had only a three-inch gap to work with. It was my only option for a shot, and knowing how well the bow was shooting, I didn't hesitate. With the bull angling away, all felt surprisingly calm, despite the pandemonium of simultaneously having three bulls within bow range.

Holding steady, the Admiral seemed to quietly release itself, sending an arrow through the tiny gap in the trees. The broadhead found its mark, entering over the right hind quarter of the bull, driving through the liver and left lung and sticking into the ground on the opposite side. A massive blood trail left no question as to the hit.

Personally, this hunt marked two firsts. It was the first time I'd had so many elk surround my calls on a single hunt. It was also the first big game animal ever taken with BowTech's Admiral.

While taking care of the bull, the sounds of others bugling across distant hillsides helped pass the time. As we rode the horses out of the hills under the cover of darkness, the closer we drew to camp, the louder the bugles became.

After tending the horses, a hearty dinner followed in the main cabin. Other hunters had gotten elk, too, and vivid stories were relived by all that night. It was a good day. A great day. In fact, it was one of the best days of elk hunting in my entire life. Never had I heard or seen so many bulls in a single day.

Before it was over, more than 20 bulls would approach to within bow range, several others hung on the outskirts. Most were brought in by seductive cow calls while a few did respond to the occasional bugle. The combination of cow calls I relied on came from the Mini Mouth and the Last Call, a custom made open-reed call crafted from cow horn. On four elk hunts that year, I called in 49 bulls to within 40 yards, and all were captured on film for our Game Chasers TV show.

My B.C. elk, skinned, quartered and heading out of the hills. For a closer look at the memorable bull, see the front cover of this book.

With the excitement of the hunt so fresh in my mind, sleep would not come easy. It didn't help when the valley lit up with bugling bulls. Then again, I wouldn't have preferred it any other way. Sleep can be made up; elk hunting experiences as special as this may only come but once in a hunter's lifetime.

Chapter 7:

Golden State Boars

I've been fortunate to hunt pigs in several places, including multiple states and six countries. Though I've had many close encounters over the years, the wild hogs of California win top billing as the most aggressive I've faced.

We could hear the band of pigs grunting and snorting as they nonchalantly fed their way through a brushy poison oak thicket. It was too dense for us to follow, so my buddy and I moved ahead of the herd, hoping to intercept them.

I stayed high on the ridgeline, my buddy dropped 100 yards below me. I sat on a well-used trail (mistake #1), surrounded by brush (mistake #2) with my best view being up and down the trail. I could see a small, grassy opening where I'd hoped the pigs would pop into, and that was my only shooting window.

A few short minutes later, I could hear the foraging herd moving my way. I was near Red Bluff, California, it was spring, and the leaves were growing thick on the trees and bushes. Getting a clear shooting lane was tougher than I'd anticipated.

The first pigs I saw–barely more than 20 yards away–scurried through the small clearing too quickly for a shot. More animals continued meandering along the same pathway, so I put my arrow back in the quiver, preparing to follow them the moment the final pig passed by.

As the last pig–or what I thought was the last pig–passed, I stood and took a step forward, down the trail. At that instant a 150-pound sow stepped in to the same trail. The second she saw me, she didn't hesitate. Ears back, bristles on her neck and shoulders erect, she came full-charge.

It was so brushy I had nowhere to turn. I knew I wasn't going to outrun her and given the fact she was closing the distance so fast, there was no way to nock an arrow and pull-off a shot.

Before I knew it she was on me, and though I tried jumping as high as I could, hoping to straddle her as she passed, she threw her head and caught the toe of my right boot. The next thing I saw was both feet surrounded by blue sky, then I hit the earth with a resounding thud.

I popped to my feet as quick as possible, ready to take another charge. Fortunately, the hog kept running down the trail.

That was my first experience hunting California hogs, and the excitement has never stopped. Since that time I've been on several pig hunts and can't get enough of them. Not only are they thrilling animals to hunt, but they offer some of the best eating wild game in the country, something my family loves.

I've been fortunate to hunt wild hogs in six different countries and multiple states. I rank California's pigs as the most aggressive I've faced.

After the charge, I joined my buddy who'd heard the commotion. When I told him what happened, he told me how lucky I was it wasn't a boar. He went on to tell me the story of how another hunter, only a couple years prior, got caught in the same predicament in the same drainage we hunted. The hog he faced was a big boar, with long, sharp tusks.

When the hunter jumped to clear the charging pig, he spread his legs in an attempt to clear the boar. Right then, the boar lifted and thrashed his head, slicing through the pants and both femoral arteries of the hunter. He died in a matter of seconds.

California's boars are some of the meanest, most aggressive big game animals I've hunted anywhere, and they're not to be taken lightly. Facing them with a bow, on the ground, is one of hunting's great thrills.

Though the conditions can be miserably hot, summer is one of my favorite times to spot-and-stalk California's hogs. At this time in the Redding and Red Bluff areas where I've done most of my hunting, daytime temperatures can reach 115°, but this can work to the hunter's advantage.

When conditions are so intensely hot, pigs feed at night, then seek shaded bedding areas by day. On the rare occasion when nighttime temperatures cool, say into the 70s, bands of pigs can be seen moving from feeding to bedding areas at the first hint of light. Other times, you have to put in the legwork to discover where their bedding areas are by following tracks.

In summer, the many creekbeds carving their way through the parched landscape are dry and haven't seen moisture for months. Given the course soil composition of the region, the creekbeds are deeply carved into the earth. In some areas it's not uncommon to have the creek bottom lay 10 to 20-yards below normal ground level.

Because these creeks are one of the few places moisture collects during the winter and early spring months, vegetation grows thick along the banks. In summer the brush is fully-leaved, and given the recessed setting of the creekbeds, this makes for the ideal shaded bedding area. Some of the deep, well-shaded creekbeds will be a good 20° cooler than open ground.

My favorite way to hunt this time of year is by tracking. It's an old-school approach, something many people have lost the skill of over the years when it comes to Western big game hunting. This is where hunting pigs can keep that skill honed, especially during the off-season.

Ideally, I like cutting tracks leading into a creek bottom, then follow them. Sometimes the big boars split from the herd, sometimes they proceed deeper into the head-end of the draws. I try to find big tracks and stick with them. Then again, sometimes I just take the opportunities as they come.

On one heart-pounding hunt I'd cut the tracks of over 20 hogs. They'd come off a dry, grassy hillside, crossed a dry, open river bed then marched into a narrow, brush-choked creekbed. I followed the tracks for over 300 yards before I caught up with the herd.

Through dense brush I could hear and see two black pigs rolling in moist, cool dirt. They were active, making plenty of noise, and the wind was good, but the brush was too dense to lace an arrow through. Moving closer, I quietly stalked to within 15 yards, but still had no shot.

Knowing there was no chance of getting an arrow through the tangled vines, I backed out of the creek and circled around from above. By the time I got to where I'd last seen pigs, they were bedded down. I looked over a few smaller hogs, then found a good boar laying against a vertical-cut bank. Not only was the angle bad, but it was hard finding his vitals, his black body blending in perfectly with the dark shade he laid in.

The big boar was just under 20 yards away, but the angle was almost straight down. Searching for another spot along the bank from which to get a shot, the moment I began to move, commotion in the creek bottom caught my attention. Two piglets were playing, running around in what looked like a game of tag.

Through the brush I could catch faint glimpses of the little bacon bits, scurrying, jumping and running about; then they headed down the creek. The minute they broke into a little clearing on an all-out sprint, I came to full-draw. My hopes were they'd awake the sleeping boar, and that's exactly what happened.

In fact, one of the piglets nearly collided with the napping hog, which brought him to his feet. Twirling as he stood, watching the piglets pass, he simultaneously gave me a perfect broadside shot. He didn't know what hit him.

As the arrow passed through his thick hide, he flinched, then ran down the creekbed, vanishing in the dense brush. Looping back into the creek bottom, I got in the brushy draw and soon found my prize, piled-up on the sandy soil.

After strapping the 225-pound boar to the quad, I soon met up with a buddy who was looking for pigs in the same area. He had a couple hounds, and I'm always up for a good chase.

On our way back to the truck to skin my boar, the dogs went ballistic. Letting the dogs loose, the chase was on. Grabbing my bow,

I followed. Figuring the hunt would be quick, I was soon reminded of how tough these pigs are and how much ground they can cover.

Up one hill and into another valley we ran, trying to keep up with the hounds. Drenched with sweat, I figured they'd bay the hog in the creek bottom. Wrong. Instead, the hog ran a couple hundred yards up the creek and buried itself in a thick patch of poison oak. There was no prayer of threading an arrow through that mess.

Eventually the dogs rooted out the pig and the chase was again on. Up and over another hill they went, but this time we caught up with them. The pig had bayed-up along the wet edges of a livestock pond and wasn't moving.

The dogs gave me plenty of shooting space, and though I'm always nervous about taking any animal with a bow when dogs are involved,

This massive boar and good sow made
my day on a hunt near Red Bluff, California.

my buddy assured me the dogs would avoid the arrow. Should the arrow be sticking out the side of the animal, the last thing I want is for an aggressive dog to run into an exposed broadhead.

At 25 yards the pig gave me the angle I needed. Tucking my sightpin tight behind the shoulder, I touched my release, sending the arrow on its way. Swiftly, the arrow passed through the hog, skipping across the rock-hard dirt on the opposite side. Rather than run, the pig retreated into the water near where it stood, making the recovery easy. I went home with two great eating hogs from that trip.

On another action-packed hunt, houndsman, Clint Arrowsmith, felt confident he could round us up a good hog. We were near Red Bluff, in the middle of winter. When using dogs, hogs are easier to trail this time of year as the scent stays on the ground longer, and the cool temperatures aren't as demanding on the hounds.

Right out of the gate the dogs were on chase. Trailing them through thick brush across a hillside, the herd moved ahead at a fast clip. As the bawls of the pack grew faint, I knew it was going to be a while until we caught them, but we kept running, hoping to close the gap.

As we ran by a small, deep rill, I glanced down at it. Stunned, I was speechless to find a big belted hog tucked tight into the head of the depression. It stood four yards from me.

The hog had obviously pulled away from the chase and ducked into the little cut without the dogs knowing it. Nocking an arrow, the pig looked me straight in the face. It was a steep bank, and though I didn't fear a charge, I knew I'd have to get a shot off, quick, for there was no telling how long the pig would stay put.

The hog's uplifted chin gave me the window I needed to slip an arrow into its throat. At the shot, the arrow buried up to the fletch, penetrating into the vitals. The pig went three steps and fell over. On its way in, the broadhead hit the jugular vein, making for a fast end.

The black and white striped pig, the prized belted hog, is what many hog hunters yearn for. I was fortunate to stumble upon this one, almost literally.

The best part about pig hunting in California is that it can be done year-round, with a variety of strategies. Be it spot-and-stalk, sitting over water holes, using predator calls or chasing hounds, there's never an end to the joy and rewards these animals provide.

A belted hog and big-toothed boar...what more could you ask for?

The fact pigs are the second most hunted big game animal in North America–behind whitetail deer–speaks wonders to their credibility. Once you face them, bow in-hand, and get some of their divine eating meat for the pot, you'll be wanting more.

Chapter 8:

Rattled Blacktail

My whitetail hunting buddies still give me grief over my decision to leave a record book buck in hopes of arrowing a blacktail...my blacktail buddies are still congratulating me for making the right choice!

"You'd better get home," urged my wife, Tiffany. "I just saw a big buck chasing a doe up in the hills."

At the time I received her call on the cell phone, I was sitting in a whitetail stand in the southeast corner of Montana. I'd seen a monster whitetail on the first evening of the hunt, and intended on holding out for him. I guessed him to go 175-inches, making him worth waiting for.

But the more I thought about it, the more the allure of a big blacktail buck beckoned me. Tiffany is a good judge of blacktails, as she grew up hunting and watching them. I knew the chances of finding that exact buck weren't all that high, but it told me the blacktail rut was on, and I didn't want to miss it.

The next whitetail that popped into view, I shot. He was a dandy 10-point, 22-inches wide, but he wasn't anything near the buck I saw two days prior. With the meat cut and packed into a cooler, I was on a plane home the very next morning.

Living where we do, in the foothills of Oregon's Cascade Range, there are both resident blacktail bucks and bucks that move down from higher elevations during the rut to inspect does. Rarely do I see the same buck twice in these densely forested mountains, but if there is a hot doe and the competition is high among mature bucks, they will hang in an area for several days.

In the foothills of the Cascades, both resident and migratory bucks can show up any time during the late season.

That evening I had less than an hour to hunt, so wasted no time heading into the hills, rattle bag and decoy in-hand. It was mid-November, marking Oregon's popular late archery blacktail season.

Working down a ridge of 40 to 50 year old Douglas firs, I looked to rattle into the brush-choked draw to the east, where Tiffany last saw the buck chasing a doe.

Propping the 3D decoy amid some lush, green ferns, I settled-in and started rattling. Nothing came in that night, and I decided to leave the decoy overnight rather than pack it out.

At daylight the following morning, I was back in the same spot, or so I thought. All looked right, except my decoy was gone. I knew it hadn't been stolen, for no one would have gone in there in the middle of the night, unless they were watching me the night before.

I looked around the ferns and found my decoy, actually my 3D target, laying in four pieces. Hoof prints were carved deep into the wet forest floor and the backside of the decoy was covered in blood. It was clear a buck had paid visit in the night, but was it the buck I was after?

I rattled for a couple hours that morning but nothing came in. During the day I walked many of the surrounding ridges and valleys, searching for pockets of does. My intent was to relocate does I'd seen during pre-season scouting missions, hoping bucks would be with them.

I covered a couple miles and saw nothing but small bucks and a few does here and there. With daylight dwindling, I dropped down in elevation, heading back toward the draw where my decoy had been demolished.

I didn't make it to my designated spot before a pair of does caught my eye. They were walking up a draw and a small buck was dogging them. Breaking out the rattle bag, I figured I'd see if I could pull any other bucks from the woods. The first time I hit the bag, the little three-point stopped, looked up the hill and pranced right in. No other buck followed.

Once the young buck moved off, I continued dropping in elevation. There were other meadows I'd been watching does feed in during late afternoon, so wanted to scan their edges in the waning hours of daylight.

The first grassy draw revealed nothing. But on the edge of the second small clearing I saw a single adult doe feeding at her leisure. Tiptoeing to within 150 yards, I sat and watched. As minutes passed, the doe grew increasingly nervous. She kept looking back into the woods, ears erect, legs stiff. She was obviously tense, but for what reason?

There had been some cougars hunting these same ridges, and coyotes were never far away. Was it predators that put the doe on edge, or something else?

About the time I started to move closer, another doe shot out of the woods and stood next to the doe I'd been watching. Then came a big buck. Head tight to the ground, he sniffed every footprint the doe ahead of him made. The moment the clearly mature buck stopped, rub-urinated and curled his lips in the air, I knew I had to make a move.

Checking the wind one last time, it was perfect, still rolling down the hill. This meant I could keep to the same ridgeline I was on, drop down closer to the deer, and try calling the buck across the opening.

The forest floor was wet, its soft, thick moss making for quiet going. It allowed me to get within 75 yards of the deer without being seen or heard. Slipping off my pack, I grabbed the rattle bag and got comfortable between some ferns and a big fir tree.

No sooner had I gently started rattling and the buck peered into the dark timber in which I sat. Staring across the clearing, he was definitely

A year prior to this hunt, I rattled in and took a nice buck on December 1st. Once a mature blacktail is taken from an area, return there the following year, you'll likely find another big buck.

interested in my sounds. A few minutes later I hit the rattle bag again, this time a bit more aggressively. Both does began heading my direction and the buck was following. Then they stopped, 60 yards out.

The does had to cross about 40 yards of clearing, then enter the timber in which I sat. Once I saw the does were interested, I switched to a doe bleat, hoping to draw them in. As tight as the buck was sticking to the one doe, it was obvious that where she went, he was going to follow.

This handsome blacktail made leaving a Montana whitetail hunt well worth it.

It worked. No sooner had the bleats reached the does then they came trotting my direction. Arrow nocked, I sat perfectly still, waiting for them to get closer. I'd ranged a root wad at 20 yards, and the does didn't slow until they were inside that range. I had a fern marked at 15 yards, and when the does stopped there, staring my direction, I could only hope the buck would follow. He did.

At 16 yards, the black forehead of the old buck took my breath away. There are few sights in the world of hunting that send my pulse racing like when I stare a mature blacktail buck straight in the eye. The perfect shape of his orange-hued antlers, his thick chest and white throat-patch stood out amid the rich green forest.

The moment he snapped his head back on the doe's hind-end, I came to full-draw. He had no idea what was coming. Even at such close range, I'll admit the shot wasn't a slam-dunk. I was so jacked-up at what was taking place, I had to make a conscious effort to keep my 20 yard pin from drawing figure-eights on the buck.

Blacktail deer, my favorite big game animal to hunt in North America.

The instant the green pin settled behind the buck's shoulder, the bow seemed to fire itself. I remember being shocked that the bow went off, but pleased that the arrow hit the mark. A short tracking job along an easy blood trail and there was my buck, laying only a few feet from a fresh rub, which I presumed was his.

I took two bucks from that spot in two consecutive years, and it wasn't by accident. This was a high-use area, and bucks had been making rubs in this exact place for at least the past five seasons. On top of that, Deer Hair Loss Syndrome had made its way through the valley a few years prior, and though doe populations were down, buck numbers were high. The fact mature bucks survive this syndrome leaves a high ratio of bucks to does, and the rattling and calling in these areas can be red-hot.

A few days later my buddy from Montana called. "The neighbor kid shot your big whitetail," he shrieked. "He went just over 180-inches!"

"That's great, good for him," I smirked. "My blacktail went 126-inches. Looks like I made the right choice to fly home early."

Chapter 9:

Horseback Bison

Since boyhood, the American bison has intrigued me. Brought back from the brink of extinction, this icon of the American West is one of North America's greatest conservation success stories. Having the opportunity to hunt them, on horseback, surpassed even my wildest dreams.

For nearly a decade, while living in Alaska's Arctic, I got used to the annual rejection notice of failing to draw a bison permit. For years I applied in Wyoming and Utah, also without success. Bison tags are one of the toughest to draw in the U.S., as I was learning, first-hand. Intent on hunting bison sooner rather than later, I turned to private ground in South Dakota, near the quaint town of Buffalo, nonetheless.

The first time I met Scott Peterson, owner of the famed Jumpoff Buffalo Ranch, he assured me it wouldn't be an easy hunt on his nearly 10,000 acres of ground, especially with a bow. He also promised to show me some of the most historic Native American bison hunting grounds in North America.

Saddling the horses, we were soon heading across the sage flats and into the rugged cliffs where the bison, or American buffalo, roamed freely thousands of years ago. No words were needed, nor desired. I was content letting my imagination run wild in this captivating landscape.

The closer the horses took us toward the badlands habitat, the larger the buffalo jump off grew. Reaching the base of the jump off, where thousands of buffalo had been driven to their death by generations of Lakota peoples, was a surreal experience.

Riding on horseback where Native American Indian peoples used to chase bison, made this hunt very special.

Envisioning the Native American hunters working together, on horseback and on foot, driving massive herds of buffalo over the cliffs where we now stood, made me wonder what it was like pursuing these giants with a stick and string in those days. What bison weren't arrowed off horseback were driven over the cliffs. Most buffalo died on impact and what ones didn't were finished-off with spears and arrows.

I've spent many days afield in the northwest corner of South Dakota and have found many amazing things. Arrowheads, hide scrapers, old buffalo bones, remnants of dinosaurs and much more, keep your mind continually tuned-in to the surroundings. Over the years I've touched several species of dinosaur bones, including perfectly preserved claws from a Tyrannosaurus Rex.

Where we were hunting buffalo, a complete Thescelosaurus, nicknamed Willo, was discovered, as was an entire T-Rex skeleton. The land is rich in history, greatly adding to the hunt.

Gazing over the land it was difficult to comprehend all that had once happened there. Not only was it hard to imagine what dinosaurs must have looked like carrying out their daily lives, but to see herds of buffalo so vast that it took people days to ride past a single herd, must have been a sight to behold.

In 1600, an estimated 60 million bison roamed North America. By 1890 they were nearly extinct. Today, over 500,000 buffalo exist, only about 15,000 of which inhabit wild, free-range land. While some privately owned ranches raise buffalo for their much desired, high-quality meat, others offer opportunities for hunters. Were it not for these private land opportunities, many hunters would never experience a bison hunt.

Honestly, I didn't know what to expect on the hunt. I figured we'd hop on the horses, ride out, find a buffalo, make a stalk and put an arrow in him. I was wrong.

The first bull we spotted was bedded on the bottom of the valley floor, some three-quarters of a mile from where we sat on our horses. We were high atop the jump off, and taking the horses over the edge was not an option. Tying off the horses, we left them on top while we hiked down the cliffs toward the bedded bull.

Picking our way through the maze of hard, gumbo outcroppings and cacti, we finally reached the bottom. Using the many cut banks and undulating land we were able to close within 100 yards of the bull.

Bison, a true symbol of the American West, are North America's largest land animal.

It was then we discovered he wasn't one we wanted. He was a very old bull, which would have made a great trophy for the wall, but I wanted something a bit younger, something that would make better eating.

Hiking back up to the horses we soon found another bull. The instant this one busted us from over 500 yards away, he took off on a sprint across the open plains. The last we saw of him he was still going, well over a mile away, nothing more than a trail of dust confirming he was still on the move.

By now it was midday, and figuring the hunt would have ended, my stomach began to growl. I didn't bother packing my lunch along. You'd think I would have learned that lesson after so many years.

Around 2:00 we were back on the daunting ridges of the buffalo jump, glassing. After some serious searching we found three bachelor bulls feeding in the bottom of a ravine. This time we lead the horses down a negotiable hillside, carefully picking our way through the broken ground.

The trio of bulls fed atop a grassy knoll and given the depth of the cut banks surrounding them, it looked like getting within bow range

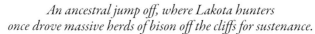

*An ancestral jump off, where Lakota hunters
once drove massive herds of bison off the cliffs for sustenance.*

was going to be easy. Slowly, quietly I watched my every step on the hard, crumbling dirt. There wasn't a breath of wind in the bottom of that canyon and it seemed the slightest of sounds was going to give me away at any moment.

Tucked out of sight from the buffalo for a good distance of the stalk, the first time I poked my head above the cut bank, I nearly gasped aloud. I couldn't believe how close they were. Scott and my camera man, Bret Stuart, stayed back, watching from a distance.

Hidden beneath the vertical bank, I nocked an arrow. Palming my rangefinder, I was certain the reading would be 20 yards, not much farther. When the reading came back as 45 yards, I didn't believe it. Two more times I hit the closest bull with the rangefinder and each time confirmed the distance at 45 yards. These animals were much larger than I'd anticipated, which threw me when estimating their distance.

Confident at that distance, I brought my bow to full-draw and slowly rose over the edge of the bank. When I popped up, one of the bulls was staring right at me. In no time flat the bulls were off and running. As I helplessly watched, they disappeared behind a ridge. Meeting back up with Scott and Bret, I was frustrated with my bonehead mistake.

Hopping on the horses, we rode around the ridgeline and were pleased to find the bulls grazing some 500 yards away. Wasting no time, Bret and I commenced another stalk in a deep-cut ravine while Scott stayed behind.

"You've got less than five minutes of filming light," reminded Bret. As if I wasn't under enough pressure, now time was limited. Picking up the pace, Bret and I quickly covered ground.

Seeing the backs of all three bulls, I once again nocked an arrow then took a reading on the range finder. Fifty yards.

Anchoring my BowTech Allegiance, I put the 50 yard pin behind the bull's shoulder. Steadying the middle pin smack in the center of his body, where the long hair met the short hair, I barely touched my release.

In the waning light, the white vanes on the Gold Tip arrow were instantly consumed by the buffalo's dark pelage. Set at 82 pounds and shooting over 320 feet-per-second, the arrow drove clean through the bull. In fact, the three of us looked for that arrow and never did find it.

All three bulls took off at the shot. The hit bull was gushing vast amounts of blood from his mouth and nose, so much in fact, we had

*A well-placed arrow at 50 yards saw this giant bull traveling
a short distance before expiring.*

to edit out a good portion of it for the TV show. Never, in all my years
of hunting had I seen so much blood lost by an animal. Seventy yards
from where he was hit, the bull collapsed, proving how lethal even a tiny
arrow is on such a massive bodied animal.

Approaching the bull, in awe of the blood trail and how quickly he
expired, I could only wonder what the Native Americans who used to
hunt these beasts with handmade, obsidian arrowheads and stick bows
would have thought. Yes, modern technologies have greatly impacted
our world, even the world of bowhunting.

I'd taken moose before, as well as some big critters in Africa,
but standing over this massive buffalo, I didn't know where to start.
Measuring 12-feet long, six-feet at the shoulders and weighing a ton, we
had our work cut out for us. Thankfully we had good, sharp knives. I
couldn't imagine skinning one of these beasts with an obsidian tool.

The memories of the hunt were everything I'd ever dreamed of, and
then some. Simply setting foot in such a land, so rich in culture and
history, was a great honor, an honor that surpassed the outcome of the
hunt, itself.

Chapter 10:

Big Sky Pronghorns

I never tire of bowhunting pronghorns.
The setting, their keen instincts and the fact they force you to
always be thinking, means they make you a better hunter.
I've learned a great deal about bowhunting, in general, during
my years of pursuing pronghorns in Big Sky country.

It was day six of the mid-August hunt. High-noon, 103° outside—who knows what the mercury would registered inside the black walls of the popup blind. At this point, even the stagnant water hole in front of me looked inviting. Watching ducks, shorebirds, turtles and other wildlife relish in the water, I'd just have to dream.

More than I wished I could be frolicking in the water, I yearned for a pronghorn buck to appear. On the first day of the hunt, a buddy arrowed a dandy buck as it came to drink at another water hole. Early in the morning of the second day, another friend got a Pope & Young buck. Here I was, six days later, figuring I'd have been tagged-out by now.

But as so often happens when I'm in the field, once I lay eyes on a big animal, I have trouble putting my tag on anything lesser. During my six days in the blind, I only left twice to relieve myself. Routinely, I was in the blind by 4:00 a.m., out at 9:00 p.m. They were long days, for sure.

On the hottest day, I didn't bring enough water and lost 11 pounds. It was 107° that day, putting it close to 120° inside the blind, I'm sure. What we hunters endure sometimes makes me question our sanity, and though it makes us stronger, I'd not recommend this experience to anyone.

It's big bucks like this that keep me passing up smaller ones.

Truth is, I love sitting over waterholes. It's like hunting from treestands in that you get to be an unseen guest in a wild setting. Being able to observe wildlife as it behaves naturally is the best learning tool. Having been a biology teacher for 12 years prior to embarking upon a full-time outdoor career, I would have loved to have my students observe wildlife around a waterhole. What they would have seen greatly surpassed anything I could teach them second-hand or from a book.

On day seven of the hunt, temperatures were supposed to be close to 110°. My camera man wasn't thrilled. Though I'd been seeing bucks every day, the 80-incher I'd had my mind set on, just wouldn't come in. One morning he came to drink at 4:30 a.m., and I could barely see him under the glow of the pre-dawn light. I saw him almost every day, and others that I should have shot that were well over the record book minimum, but the big guy never came into range.

Pouring with sweat and nearly out of sunflower seeds and water, when a small buck started working our way, I told the camera man we were going to take him. It was the first time I'd seen him smile in a week. It was also one of the smallest bucks we'd had come in, but it was time to end this hunt.

At 15 yards, the shot was simple, and my BowTech Tribute did the job. The buck went 20-some yards, stopped, wobbled, and fell over. As we watched him take his final kicks in the hot, dry dirt, two other bucks approached the water hole. One was a small buck, one was bigger. Much bigger.

The bigger buck, having seen mine fall, came in on a dead run, stopping to inspect the scene. Then he walked right in front of us and drank. I guessed him at 74 inches. A buddy killed the buck later that year, with a rifle. He went 76 inches. Had I waited five more minutes to launch an arrow, I likely would have had that brute. I now had reason to return the following year.

I love this early archery hunt in eastern Montana. The tag is guaranteed, even for nonresidents, and the season kicks-off well ahead of other bowhunts out West. Never have I run in to another hunter, not even a resident.

The following year I returned and was hunting with good friend, Shane Weiler. Shane was born and raised in Forsyth, Montana, near where we were hunting, and had taken a liking to bowhunting during my experience the year prior. Setting him up with a brand new Diamond bow, he was shooting lights-out, eager to hunt his first animal with a bow.

The first day in the blind nothing came in. We saw some good bucks but they quit using the water in front of us. Cattle had come in during the night, mucked up the water, and the antelope would have nothing to do with it. Shane and I moved the blind into the next little draw, situating it 20 yards from a tiny seep.

There was only a little water at this spot but it was clear and clean. The only thing to catch the water and hold it were a few old cow prints that sank deep into the ground when it was muddy. Now they were rock-hard and made perfect catch basins.

The next day, there we were, sitting in a popup blind 20 yards from a waterhole that was literally the size of a coffee cup. I learned something that day: it's not the size of the water hole, rather the quality of water inside it that antelope like.

Sure enough, at 9:00 a.m., in came two bucks. Only one would leave. The blind didn't have a single sprig of brush to conceal it, and the antelope didn't give it a second look. Over the years we've arrowed many dandy bucks after just having erected a blind. Seems antelope don't need a blind in place to get used to like deer or elk sometimes do. We've taken some good bucks after carrying in a blind, setting it up and hunting from it that morning.

Shane Weiler and his first big game animal taken with a bow. From this point on, Shane was hooked on bowhunting.

Recovering Shane's buck, he was elated. His first big game animal with a bow marked a turning point in his hunting career. Shane was loving bowhunting, and after rifle hunting for over 20 years, was excited about his new-found passion.

Prior to my arrival, Shane had been watching a whopper buck and had already put a blind at the waterhole he was using. It was a big pond, 45 yards wide, over 100 yards long, but there were a few trails antelope had been routinely using.

On the first morning of sitting in the blind, I saw the big buck, but he was leery, and never came to drink. Other, smaller bucks and several does were also edgy, some of which reluctantly came to wet their lips. Day two was a repeat of day one–lots of animals but all overly cautious.

Not sure what was wrong, Bret Stuart, my camera man, stayed in the blind while I popped up on the hill to look over the waterhole from above, at the same angle the pronghorns were approaching from. We figured they didn't like coming in from above and having to drink from a waterhole that sat in a depression, whereby making it difficult for them to see approaching predators.

That may have been part of the answer, but when I reached the top of the hill, I found the real truth. I could see right through the blind. Bret didn't even have to move and I could clearly see his body outline. As we moved around in the blind, looking through binoculars, rangefinders and the TV camera, we could only imagine what the animals were seeing.

It hadn't even caught my attention, but when I crawled back into the blind, it dawned on me that inside it wasn't black. Black material is used inside ground blinds to block out the light. Without the black, too much light passes through the blind, revealing your presence. We packed up that blind and sent it back to the factory.

The next day Bret and I would be sitting in another blind and I'd fill my tag. It was 102° that day. Right then and there, we committed to coming back the following season. Our Big Sky pronghorn hunts were fast becoming tradition.

I held out for a giant buck I'd been seeing, but settled for this one on the last day. Still, this buck carried enough horn to make the record books.

The following August, I wanted to do something different, so I hunted over a tiny watering hole from a treestand. The brushy tree was a joy to sit in after roasting for so many days in ground blinds on previous hunts, but only one doe came to water. After three days, I moved to an abandoned outhouse near an old homestead, where water lightly seeped from the ground. Two days there was enough.

Day six was spent back in a pop-up blind, and though a couple smaller bucks came in, nothing was worth shooting. Sitting in a blind was wearing on me, and I told Shane I would give it one more evening.

No sooner had we crawled into the blind and the sky turned black. Thunder and lighting rocked the hills and prairie flats. A monsoon-type downpour forced us from the blind, and back to Shane's place for the night.

The next morning the skies were still dark, but only a few faint raindrops fell. However, temperatures dropped by nearly 60 degrees and it was downright cold. Given the wet, cold conditions, we decided to go spot-and-stalk on day seven.

This part of southeast Montana is not really built for stalking antelope, but eager for a change, we decided to give it a try. From far atop a ridge, Shane spotted a herd of bachelor bucks, and though I tried, there were simply too many eyes to try and fool. That was a bummer, as there were some whopper bucks in that group.

Then we spotted two bucks grazing in a freshly cut alfalfa field. We were in one pasture that had just been baled; the bucks were on the edge of another that had been cut, but not yet baled. "If you get low and work behind those bales of hay, I bet you can pull it off," Shane smiled. Always up for a challenge, I headed across the field with my camera man in tow.

Covering the first 600 yards was easy, but as I drew closer the bales became sparse. Then I saw a tiny ditch, that, if I crawled into, would cover me just enough to reach the next bale. It worked. Now I was within 85 yards of the feeding bucks.

On hands and knees I crawled to the last bale which put me 55 yards from the bucks. Ahead of me was a fenceline, grown over with tall weeds and alfalfa the baler couldn't reach. That was the break I needed.

Inching to the edge of the fence I found a hole in the weeds and hit the closest buck with my rangefinder. At 43 yards, it was now or never. Coming to full-draw, I stood, barely clearing the brush in the fenceline.

Smoothly, the BowTech General–still one of my favorite bows of all-time–silently sent the Gold Tip arrow on its way.

The buck went less than 100 yards before tumbling on the edge of the alfalfa field. Reaching to pull his head from a windrow of alfalfa, I was shocked, for he was much larger than I thought. Honestly, I never did pay much attention to his headgear, as I was so focused on making the stalk. It just turned out that he'd be one of my better speedgoats taken with a bow.

After several days of sitting in a blind, spot-and-stalk proved to be the way to go. The conditions were perfect to stalk on this big buck.

One stalk, one record book buck. That beat sitting at a waterhole in miserable heat for days on end.

Shane was up next, and as we were driving back to his place to take care of my buck, we spotted a lone buck bedded one-third of the way down the south-facing slope of a small hill. "I can get him," was all Shane said.

Shane is on the list of some of my favorite people to hunt with. He lives, eats and breathes hunting and always has his mind tuned-in to doing things that will help improve himself. His newfound love of bowhunting is his testimony.

Backing up the truck so as not to spook the buck, I sat and watched while Shane commenced stalking. It took him less than 10 minutes to reach the hill the buck was on, as he didn't want him to stand and move off.

Finally, when I saw Shane's head pop above the skyline, I knew he was close. I could clearly see both the buck and Shane, but Shane could not yet see the buck bedded below him. Then, Shane drew his bow and slowly stood.

The instant Shane stood, so did the buck, and I saw Shane release. The buck took off over a hill and disappeared. Shane held the bow over his head, confirming a good hit.

Coming together at his buck, Shane and I were again taken by it's size. Two stalks in less than an hour and we had two Pope & Young pronghorns on the ground. Shane explained that the buck was bedded tight behind a bush, and there was no way he could get a shot unless the buck stood. It was a risky move, but Shane played it smart and made a perfect shot.

That afternoon, after getting our bucks hung in a cold locker, Shane and I set out for some fun, chasing prairie dogs. This had become another tradition of ours, shooting high volumes of arrows in the many prairie dog towns of the area. In fact, one day we filmed an entire show, bowhunting prairie dogs for BowTech's Western Adventures. To this day, of the more than 300 TV episodes I've filmed, that could be the one which we've received the most feedback on. People loved it and learned a lot.

"I had no idea you could get so close to prairie dogs," was the number one remark we heard. They are a great animal for bowhunters to hone their overall skills on. From stalking to judging distance, from shooting in various positions to learning how the wind effects arrow flight, there is so much to be learned from actually shooting at animals under real hunting conditions.

Sometimes we'd shoot judos, but usually we relied on our practice broadheads. This allowed us to truly evaluate the performance of our gear. With thousands of prairie dogs to shoot at, the only thing that put an end to our fun was how fatigued our bodies became after flinging hundreds of arrows.

Shortly after filling my tag, Shane Weiler made a great stalk on this buck. Two stalks, two Pope & Young class bucks; it doesn't get any better.

Hunting prairie dogs in early fall is one of the best ways to experience high-volume shooting at live animals in real hunting conditions.

Whenever I go on a hunt where I know there will be prairie dogs or jack rabbits, I bring along plenty of extra arrows and old broadheads. Of all the forms of practicing I do, the practical experience of stalking, ranging and shooting at live game, in real situations, has taught me the most. I always look forward to such fun, educational shoots. The ranchers are usually happy to see us, too, helping rid their grounds of the unwanted rodents.

Incidentally, on the prairie dog hunt we filmed, I was shooting in high winds that reaffirmed my belief in the staggered vane setup I use, and have been using for years. I'll detail this setup, and it's value, in the final chapter, Closing Thoughts.

Chapter 11:
Roosevelt Redemption

Pursuing Roosevelt elk is an experience every archer must live. Only then will true appreciation of their behaviors, the rugged country they call home and everything else that separates them from their Rocky Mountain cousins, be realized.

Two hours of calling and finally the bull started moving my direction. Good friend and noted guide, Jody Smith, and I caught him in a large meadow with nearly 20 cows. We didn't think we had a prayer of pulling him away from his harem, but there was nowhere else to move. We had no choice but to give it a try.

It was the last of a five day hunt, and though we'd called in some respectable bulls–six to be exact–none were what I was looking for. Finally, we had the bull of my dreams headed our way.

Over the course of that two hours we heard more cow chatter than most hunters hear in an entire season. We also witnessed our bull being challenged by two other bulls, one of which was considerably bigger than the one climbing the hill to check out our calls.

Every time our bull started moving toward us, another bull would sneak in and try to steal a cow. Then our bull would forget about us and run off the challenger. One time he chased a 320-inch monster bull across the meadow, through a 300 yard wide thicket of 20 year old Douglas fir, then straight up the steep face of a logged unit. In all, the bull covered three-quarters of a mile before driving the challenger out of sight.

When our bull appeared on the ridge, he ran just as quickly back to his harem. He was tired, breathing hard and totally focused on his cows.

After taking a drink from a small spring, he mounted a receptive cow. After the third mating, he was content.

We hit the calls again, TV cameras rolling, catching all the action. Finally, the bull started moving back up the hill, right toward us. By now, daylight was quickly fading. If he didn't cover the next 250 yards in under five minutes, we'd be out of filming light.

The bull kept moving our way, but was in no rush. He bugled at nearly every mew and bugle we threw his way, but we just couldn't get him to pick up the pace. He'd already gotten in two fights, and was leery about leaving his cows unattended.

Usually quiet, when Roosevelt bulls start talking, optimism runs high in hunting camp.

Finally, he tipped his massive rack across his wide back and let out a deep, rough-throated bugle. He turned, looked our way, then started moving uphill, right at us. Every time he stopped, I cow called in an effort to get him to budge. The high-pitched sounds seemed to get him the most excited.

With less than two minutes of filming light left, he was still over 100 yards out. We were looking into the wide open meadow, a small fir tree at our backs. Fifty more yards was all I wanted.

Slowly, the bull kept coming, but by the time he got within range, it was too late. I could have shot the bull several times between 40 and 50 yards, but when we lost camera light, I quit calling. I just sat there, watching the bull, hoping he wouldn't bust me so that maybe we could find him some other day.

Though I'd quit calling, the bull kept coming. At 28 yards, it was almost more than I could handle. Here I was, face-to-face with a massive, black-maned bull pushing 300 inches–the biggest Roosevelt I'd ever called in–and I couldn't shoot. For more than two minutes he stood there, most of it broadside. He wasn't as big as one of the bulls he'd chased off, but there was no question he was the herd bull.

It's times like this I'm not real fond of shooting TV shows. After two hours of work, the bull was in my lap, yet it was too dark to shoot. Too dark for the camera, that is. I could have shot him over and over again during the final 10 minutes of legal shooting light. But I stuck to our rule…"No kill on film, no TV show!"

Intently, the monarch searched for the calling cow and younger bull. At times it felt like he was staring right through me. Then, ever so slowly, the bull turned and melted into the darkness, heading back down the hill to his harem. We never saw him again.

Many of the pleasures we hunters enjoy come from friends we make along the way. From the time I first met Jody Smith, we hit it off. He's one of the hardest working, most knowledgeable men I've had the honor of hunting with. His humble ways and honest nature are a true testimony to what kind of man he is. He's the kind of guy I want my sons to grow up and be like. The world of hunting could use more people like Jody.

Outgoing, positive and always fun to be with, over the years I've filmed more TV shows with Jody Smith than anyone in the world. He's wonderful to be around; both of my boys and wife love him and his family, too. Every spring and fall, I look forward to filming hunts with Jody.

Although we never saw the big bull again, we didn't give up. The following day I had to fly to South Dakota for a scheduled antelope hunt, but returned home a few days later, having filled that tag. Jody only lives an hour from me, and the next day we met-up for a one day elk hunt. I had only one day, as I was soon to board another plane, this one to Alaska in search of brown bear.

We knew it was a long shot, but we also knew I couldn't fill a tag if we didn't at least try. Jody and I went back to where we'd seen the big bull, but couldn't find him or his cows.

That morning was slow, but in the middle of the afternoon the action heated up. Jody and I worked a section of 40 year old fir trees, on public land. The first cow sound I let out received a bugle from above us. Again I called, and again got a bugle. He was close, within 150 yards.

Focusing our attention up the hill, where the bull could be heard, we listened. Jody sat 10 yards behind me. His ears and eyes are as good as anyone's I've hunted with, and when he pointed down over the hill, then cupped his ear, I knew he heard another bull approaching.

Roosevelts are not as vocal as Rocky Mountain bulls, and are notorious for coming in silent. In fact, of all the Roosy's I've called in over the years, well over half have come in without making a sound. That's what makes hunting them such a rush, but at the same time, so frustrating.

Then I heard it. Tchhh...Tchhh...Tchhh...Tchhh. The sound of hooves quickly beating across the noisy forest floor was clear. When the lone bull popped into view, I knew I'd have to shoot him. For one, time was limited, and we needed to put a bull on the ground if we were to get a TV show. Second, even if the bull bugling on the hill above us was the big bull, I didn't want the approaching bull to bust us and possibly ruin everything.

The bull came in on a string, straight at us, never slowing down. When he stepped behind a tree at 15 yards, I came to full-draw. The shot was simple, driving the 100 grain broadhead and Gold Tip arrow completely through his chest.

As the five-point ran off, I quickly grabbed my cow call and let out a series of excited, high-pitch mews. The bull stopped, looked back at me, glanced at his wound and fell over, 30 yards from where I sat. Another great hunt with Jody had come to a close.

Over the years Jody and I have shared many exciting Roosevelt hunts, but my biggest bull came a year later, with just my camera man, Bret Stuart, and I. Jody and I had been hunting together for a few days, and had seen some good bulls. Then Jody booked a last minute trip with

Though I'd passed up larger ones, I settled for this bull on the last day. Jody Smith (left) is one of my absolute favorite people to hunt with.

two clients, so I headed to the west facing slopes of the Coast Range, near the town of Florence, Oregon.

No sooner had Bret and I reached a good looking gorge when we spotted a big bull across the giant canyon. He'd just popped out on to a landing, and given the layout of the logging roads, we felt we could get pretty close.

Off the edge of the steep ravine we went, stumbling over logs and through thick tangles of blackberry vines. The wind was perfect, and after nearly an hour of hiking, we pulled ourselves out of the old logged unit.

Tiptoeing down the dirt logging road, a slight breeze in our face, we rounded the corner and bumped into a good bull. He wasn't the bull we first saw, but he was a shooter, no question. The bull accompanied a half-dozen cows, and knowing we couldn't stalk any closer, our best bet was to set up and call.

At the first sweet cow sounds I offered him, he couldn't gather his cows and get off the mountain fast enough. As he crashed into the bottom of the ravine, another herd plowed through thick brush no more than 100 yards above us. Just that fast, what seemed like a slam-dunk hunt, went bad.

Not giving up, we hiked around the ridge and called into the next canyon. Immediately two bulls answered. They were close, so we got set and I called again. This time bulls bugled all around us, even across the distant canyon from where our initial stalk started. In all, we counted eight bulls bugling.

However, after 20 minutes of calling, no bulls were getting closer. They still bugled at nearly every sound I made, but none were leaving the many cows in this drainage. So, we began walking and calling. If the bulls weren't going to come to us, we were going to play their game and try to walk and talk our way into the herd.

A quick drop in temperature and a wall of gray clouds moved in from the coast. We were less than five miles from the Pacific Ocean, where weather can change in a matter of minutes. No rain came but intense thunder and lightening struck. That really got the bulls fired-up.

I'm not sure if it was the sudden drop in barometric pressure, the high number of cows in the area, the fact so many bulls were in competition with one another, or a combination of the three, but this was the most Roosevelts I'd ever heard bugling at one time. Confident we could get close for a shot, Bret and I pushed on.

There's no predicting what a big Roosevelt
bull will do or how he'll behave. The key is never giving up.

As we rounded a knoll, we saw a nice bear plucking blackberries from a vine, then he moved into the dense timber. I took my open reed call and blew some alluring animal distress sounds. Instantly the bear rambled out of the forest, ears up, searching for the source of the sounds. In short order he covered nearly 100 yards, and before I knew it, he was within bow range.

I looked at Bret, and he nodded, pointing down into the draw below. Not 200 yards away stood a big bull with about a dozen cows. We gave up on the bear and stuck to the elk.

As darkness closed in we called it a day and headed out of the canyon. Though it was the most Roosevelt' bulls I'd ever been around, I never did get within range. The next morning we were right back in there.

The storm had passed in the night and starry skies confirmed it was going to be a clear day. Given all the bulls that were talking the evening prior, I felt certain we'd pick up right where we left off.

Walking out on to the point of a ridge, I let out a perfect cow sound. I followed it with another. Not a single bull responded. Bret and I just looked at one another in disbelief. Not until 9:00 a.m. did we finally see an elk, and never did we hear one up to that point.

Sure signs big bulls are living in the area.

It was a big bull, the first bull we'd seen the afternoon prior, but failed to get on. He was across a deep canyon, over a mile from where we saw him the day before. He had some cows scattered around, but it was hard to tell how many, given the fact they were so spread out, feeding in tall, thick patches of brush.

Eventually the herd moved into a stand of timber and emerged out the bottom. When they began heading our direction, up the steep hillside, Bret and I wasted no time getting into position. If we played it right, the herd would come out on the trail we sat on.

When the elk showed up, they were 100 yards out, heading straight for us. Then the lead cow veered to the right and the herd followed. Not what we were hoping for, but at least we could now see them. The air was calm, so I let out a subtle cow chirp. Immediately a young bull lifted his head and started walking our way. Another mew, this time a drawn-out sound, and more elk started coming toward us.

Now I could see the big bull, but he wasn't following any of the younger bulls which were headed our direction. Not wanting them to get too close and give away our presence, the second the approaching bulls slipped into a little swale, Bret and I got out of there.

By now it was late morning and a steady breeze was blowing from the ocean. That's one thing I love about hunting the coast for elk; the winds are usually consistent and predictable. We could see the herd beginning to feed through a meadow, toward a thick patch of reprod', so we hiked around the ridge, got the wind in our face and commenced stalking.

Just as Bret and I poked our heads out of a brushy draw, we could see the back of an elk, less than 30 yards away. It was a small six point, and Bret wanted me to shoot it. In hindsight, I should have, but seeing as how the bull had no idea we were near, I wanted to see if our big bull was within range.

Inching forward, I couldn't believe my eyes. Within 40 yards of where Bret and I sat, hunched as low to the ground as possible, were over 20 head of elk. Beyond them were even more. Bret wasted no time rolling tape and I quit counting at 52 head. I'm sure there were more elk hidden in the brush.

The herd we'd been chasing joined another herd and all the elk were contently feeding, together. It was now high noon and warming up. By this point many hunters would have called it quits for the day, figuring the elk would be bedded down. We were glad we didn't give up.

Within minutes we had five head, noses to the ground, feeding within 15 yards of us, including that little 6x6. He was a mature bull, but there were two bigger ones feeding beyond him that I really wanted to try for. It was interesting to watch these bulls graze, knowing how rut-crazed they were the evening prior. It goes to show how sporadic rutting activity can be. Seventeen hours ago I would have bet money the rut was at it's peak. On this day, the rut seemed the farthest thing from the minds of these mature bulls.

When the elk in front of us started skirting around a bench, I knew it was only a matter of minutes before they caught our wind. Knowing I had to make a move, now it was crunch time. Opting to pass the 6x6 in front of me, I worked along the edge of the shadows, knowing he and the others with him would spook. My goal was to get a crack at one of the two big bulls.

Arrow nocked, I moved forward, cow calling as I went. The shadows were dark along the edge of the timber I worked, and helped conceal my movement. Bret stayed back, filming from beneath the bows of a cedar tree.

This is a prime example of how I don't get overly concerned if an elk sees or hears me. As long as they can't smell me, I feel I always have a chance of closing the deal. Here I was, clearly visible to more than 50 head of elk, but because I was in the shadows, moved slowly, cow called and the wind was right, they didn't run off.

As the animals grew nervous, they trotted around in confusion, but I kept cow calling. When I reached the last stand of trees on the edge of the meadow, I knew the shot would come from this spot or not at all. Had I not been calling, I'm convinced every elk would have busted out of there.

The more I called, the more curious the herd grew. I was now in a position where the elk couldn't get around to wind me. Then one of the craziest encounters I've ever had in the elk woods unfolded before my eyes.

Not only did the elk I'd spooked show interest in my continual cow chatter, but they actually started coming closer. More than 20 head had balled-up and began walking across an open meadow, right at me. All the others would soon follow. They quickly covered 25 yards and when I picked up the rangefinder and got a 60 yard reading, I knew something was going to happen.

As the herd kept closing, I let them come, sitting perfectly still in the middle of the last shadow, grass no taller than the soles of my boots. In the back of the herd I laid eyes on a giant bull, bigger than the one I was after. He was over 300-inches, but I knew I didn't have a prayer of getting him.

As the herd grew more nervous they quickened their pace and began moving away, from my left to right. Letting them go, I clinched the Last Call cow call in my teeth, waiting for the right bull to enter my line of sight. I'll never forget the image of the big 5x6 as he followed the herd, trotting with his massive headgear thrown across his back. He was one of the last to file by, and when I let out an excited cow call, he came to a screeching halt.

Hard work, persistence and patience paid-off on this massive Roosevelt bull.

I quickly ranged him at 56 yards. His huge, dark head, thick rack and deep chest left no doubt he was an old bull. Wasting no time I drew and touched the release. The BowTech Tribute sent my arrow speedily on its way. The bull didn't move a muscle, and my sturdy Gold Tip arrow buried to the vanes.

Immediately I picked up the cow call and started waling on it. The bull, along with many others in the herd, stopped. His legs were weak and he nearly tipped over right there, but managed to stagger over the edge of a brushy ravine.

Finding the bull in thick brush, I didn't want to risk

A gratifying end to a successful Roosevelt elk hunt. Pursuing wise bulls in their native Coast Range habitat is one of the West's most challenging hunts.

having him go any further into the tangled mess in the bottom of the canyon. Threading an arrow through vines and branches, I drove an insurance shot into the bull's heart. He jumped, lunged forward, went five yards and collapsed, coming to rest in the only open spot in sight.

Though he didn't carry the biggest rack we'd seen on this hunt, he was the largest bodied elk I'd ever taken, and was the bull we'd set our sights on the evening prior. I learned many lessons that day, the most important being how aggressive hunters can be and still close the deal. In this case, as has happened so many times in the elk hunting woods, I worked hard and found redemption.

One thing's for certain, and that's the fact TV has made me a better hunter. My time is usually limited on each of the hunts we go on, and with only so many days in the fall, and multiple tags to fill, we try and turn a TV show every five days or so.

This doesn't give much time, meaning we have to be aggressive, take chances and hope for the best. Such demands have made me a more complete, more efficient bowhunter, and have allowed me to experience elk hunting on a level I never knew existed.

Chapter 12:

Bruiser Bruins of Quinault

While Prince of Wales and Vancouver islands are renowned for their oversized black bears, when I first laid eyes on the bruins of the Quinault, I knew this was a special place.

As the giant bear exited the lush coastal habitat of Washington's Olympic Peninsula, my pulse raced. From the second I laid eyes on him there was no doubt the bear was an absolute giant. His waddling stride first told the story, for with each step it seemed his hind-end was going to twist forward and slap his shoulder. His thick legs retained their shape all the way to the wrists, and his mental demeanor and blockhead left no question he was an old-timer.

A shimmering, ebony pelt set him apart from the brilliant green jungle through which he emerged. As he broke out of the brush and on to a logging road along which I sat, I wasn't overly optimistic. "There's no way he's going to stay on the road and follow it all the way to where I'm sitting," I thought to myself, gripping my bow, arrow knocked.

He was in no hurry, occasionally stopping to pluck fresh grass from one side of the road, then move to the other. I pulled him from the forest with the use of hand-held predator calls and kept him coming my way by producing a variety of sounds.

I was fortunate, for it's tough calling bears in the forests of the Pacific Northwest, and this time I was able to observe how the bear was responding to my sounds. When he seemed to lose interest, I'd call some more. He was in no rush, but kept moving my way.

Ten minutes later he'd cut the distance in half, and optimism ran higher with each step he took. "Maybe there is a chance," I thought.

As the boar continued my direction, I hunkered lower behind the makeshift blind which I'd put into place just minutes before.

The rudimentary blind consisted of nothing more than a collection of 20-inch tall branches I'd snapped off and stuck in the ground in front of me. The green leaves provided the perfect cover, and the low-profile of the foliage would allow me to reach full-draw on a number of potential lanes. A backdrop of heavy brush served to further conceal me.

At 50 yards out the bear was still working in the right direction. He came from the least likely place I'd anticipated a bear to approach from, which meant his head-on position would not offer a bow shot until he was close, real close. With his head facing me, I stayed hunkered down, daring not to move and risk spooking the brute.

At four yards the bear finally paused. On my knees, I remained hunched over, prone, shaking with anticipation, already locked at full-draw. I strained to see under the bill of my cap as to what the bear's next move would be. Then the beast dipped his snout into the grassy strip in the middle of the gravel road and came up with a mouthful.

The air was still and I could hear every breath he took. Each time he closed his jaws to chew I could feel it shake through my body. His proportionally small eyes set amid a massive skull, rotated in their sockets, searching for something, likely the sounds I'd been making.

Swallowing the bite of grass, he licked his nose, smacked his lips and tilted his snout above his head, testing the wind. Chlorophyll-saturated drool ran down his lips, dripping from the crook of his mouth into his thick, black hair. He sensed all was right and started to take a step forward.

The bear had no idea I was so near and I had no intention of surprising him at such close range. I made a snap decision to twitch the bow in my hand, hoping the movement of the top limb would catch the bear's eye. Had I let the bear continue on his path, he would have been within two feet of where I sat. I did not want to be discovered at such close range with only a few twigs separating me from what I figured to be the largest black bear I'd ever seen in my life.

The moment my bow moved, the bear stopped and instantly glared at it. I was staring a Boone & Crockett bear in the eyes at 10 feet, yet I couldn't take the shot.

The bear took two steps in the opposite direction, stopped and looked back. I had the perfect double-lung shot, but the camera man perched behind me called it off, as some big leaves blocked his view. We were filming an episode for Adventures Abroad, a show I hosted during it's first season on the Outdoor Channel. We wanted it to be perfect. Unfortunately, the shot window never opened for the camera, and the bear melted into the rainforest from which he came without my firing and arrow.

There I sat, 20 minutes into the hunt and the largest bear I'd seen in my life just walked away. There's no doubt in my mind that bear was well over 500 pounds–a giant for that time of year–and would have sported a definite record book skull, likely over 22-inches. I've been fortunate to take many good bears over the years, and this, a spring bear nonetheless, was the most magnificent black bear I'd ever set eyes on. Believe me, doing so at such close range made it all the more memorable.

Before the night was over, another bear would pass within eight yards of me, one more within nine, and though both were Pope & Young animals, neither were in the same class as the first bear which approached.

Baiting is allowed on Washington's Quinault Indian Nation land. It's about the only way to get a look at the many bears roaming this dense, coastal habitat.

As daylight dwindled, movement in the brush to the left caught my eye. The bear slowly walked along a worn trail, heading right where I'd hoped. I'll never forget his stature; old in appearance, a hide beyond its prime, but a head that would have fit well on any grizzly body. For the second time, in lass than four hours, I'd seen the biggest bear of my life; his squared hide and skull, would have eclipsed that of the first bear. Then, for no apparent reason, at 60 yards out, he withdrew into the brush, never to be seen again.

Over the next five evenings I'd sit in the same blind, holding out for one of those two giants. I tried calling, but nothing else ever came to my sounds.

I caught a glimpse of the first giant one more time, as he approached a bait we'd set, but I couldn't get a shot. Then, on the last day of my hunt, I slipped an arrow tipped with a Titanium 100 grain broadhead into a dandy bear. It was the first bear I'd taken with my BowTech Allegiance. My Gold Tip Pro 400 arrow passed through the bear, and the tracking job was quick.

It was a bitter-sweet ending. I was elated at taking a very good bear, but knowing the magnitude of the bears that roamed this land, I knew, too, that I could do better. As in any big game hunting, especially with moody bears, there's no guarantee you'll ever see the animals again. When my hunt ended, it was comforting knowing that the two giants still roamed the forest, and likely many more like them. They would also serve as a calling for my return to this special place.

It was late April, 2005, and I was hunting on the Quinault Indian Nation Reservation. Not since 1855 had the reservation been open to hunting by non-tribal members, and as you would expect, the 200,000-plus acre preserve–which encompasses some 350 square miles–hosts some of the most impressive black bears on the planet. Here, hunters are required to hire tribal guides.

While the Coast Range mountains of the Pacific Northwest are teaming with black bears in many areas, seeing them is tough in this rugged, densely foliated habitat. Furthermore, food is so abundant, bears rarely need to venture into open areas, meaning random sightings can be few and far between.

But during my six day stay, I saw 23 bears, and all were boars. Of these, I estimated at least one-third to be Pope & Young bears, figuring three would have no problem making both the P&Y and Boone & Crockett Club record books.

I was the first person to film a hunt on the Quinault and write about it in national magazines. This is one of the first bears taken by a non-tribal member since 1855.

Three things set Quinault bear hunting apart from other elite bear destinations I'd been to. It's easy to access, hadn't been hunted by non-tribal members for nearly 150 years and here, within the boundaries of Reservation land, the utilization of bait is allowed–the only place in Washington where this practice is legal.

Due to the lack of hunting pressure by tribal members, bear densities were bursting to the point carrying capacities were overflowing. As a result of competition for food–and the fact many boars were keeping sows and cubs away from easy-to-access food sources–the bears lower on the chain of command had resorted to feasting on the cambium layer of both Douglas fir and cedar trees. Logging is big business on the Reservation, and with intensive studies revealing that bears are causing a conservative estimation of one-million dollars in timber loss each year, the decision was made to open the land to non-tribal hunters.

Because the habitat is so dense, the highest percentage tactical approach for hunters to take is to hunt over bait in the evening. Most guides in this area know the land extremely well, and they know where the bears den, migrate and feed. They are dialed in to their spring and summer rutting behaviors, thus know where the big boars will be cruising during breading season, as well as their fall habits which concentrate big bears near rivers and creeks.

Thanks to a relationship with a local fish processing plant that provides fresh, offshore remains, and with a store that offers expired sweets and breads, some guides have the ability to strategically place alluring bait stations in key areas. The most motivated guides start running baits in early spring, prior to the season opener, and keep them active into the fall hunting season. Combine this with the fact they closely monitor each set, and this means the Native guides can offer a high-percentage hunt for record-class bears.

How good is the Quinault? I hunted this land the first two seasons it became open to outsiders, and took two bears each time. Members of my hunting party also took bears, and some giant ones at that. I've hunted bears in various western destinations, including Alaska and Canada, and can honestly say I've never seen such a high density of big bears anywhere.

There's no question this place would give Vancouver Island and Alaska's Prince of Whales Island some serious competition, and it wouldn't surprise me if it eventually surpasses them in terms of percentages of record book entries per animal taken.

Future success is going to come down to how educated the bears become over continued years of hunting. It will also be dependent upon how hard the guides are willing to work, and how serious they take their hunting. A key to consistent success on big bears will require guides to continually reach new, unhunted lands. It may also require hunters to be willing to pass the first bears they see, whereby holding out for the big ones.

With so much food available in this rainforest setting, bears may not become conditioned to hit baits year after year. Just knowing there are so many big bears roaming the forest, this fact alone will keep hunters coming here for as long as the opportunity to hunt them remains.

Is it a slam-dunk for getting a book bear? Certainly not, no free-range hunt ever is, for any species out West that I'm aware of. But if you're patient, can judge bears and are willing to hold off on sub-par animals, I feel this place will stack-up against any of the top-producing areas of trophy bears. Again, having a guide that does his homework will also weigh on hunter success.

As with any bear hunt, it comes down to being in the right place at the right time. I've seen big bears here in less than 10 minutes of hunting. I also shared a camp with a hunter who never saw a bear. There were 12 guys in camp that week, and 11 of us killed bears, many of us took two bears. The unlucky soul simply couldn't buy a bear. I offered him my blind one night, and he passed. I took a 375 pound brute that night. I offered it to him again the following night, and again he passed. Another hunter took me up on the offer, and he took a bear over 425 pounds that evening. I moved to another blind that evening and took a very nice bear with my bow, while the hunter with an empty tag didn't see a single bruin. That's hunting; anything can happen.

Biologists running trapping surveys on the Reservation have recorded bears over seven feet in length, from nose to the base of the tail, with weights estimated to exceed 600 pounds. I know of one man whom, on his hunt, saw 18 bears one spring evening and took what was believed to be a top-ten skull. Another bear, taken a few miles from where I filled a tag, had a reported skull stretching the tape to over 22 inches. A buddy and producer of my TV show, Jim Burnworth, took two record book bears with his BowTech Old Glory in three days during the very first spring season. One of these brutes weighed over 400 pounds and carried a 21-plus-inch skull.

When hunting this coastal rainforest, the natural elements can impact the hunt, no doubt. Extended, cold winters can keep bears in

My producer, Jim Burnworth, has arrowed some monster bears on the Quinault. This spring bruin tipped the scales to over 400 pounds and squared well beyond seven feet.

their holes later than normal; mild winters may see bears emerging from their dens after only a few weeks of sleep. Weather, be it rain, cold or heat can definitely impact bear activity.

The first time I hunted the Quinault in early April, I smoked a big bear with my muzzleloader on the first day. Over the next three days, while trying to fill a second tag with a bow, I saw only two bears. One bear I estimated at nearly 400 pounds with a giant jughead, bedded down 20 yards behind me, but there was no way to thread an arrow through the brush.

I returned three weeks later to wrap-up the bowhunt. That's when I was blown away by the number of big bears I saw moving each evening. It really opened my eyes to just how magnificent the Quinault truly is. The fact I was carrying a bow, and TV cameras were once again in tow, I failed to connect on any of the three massive bears I saw that trip. One bear didn't give me a clear shot, and the other two came in after we'd lost filming light.

Shooting those two bears would have been easy, but our TV camera's lose light faster than the human eye, and if the kill shots aren't on film, we don't take them, period. Such experiences are frustrating when making outdoor television, but at the same time, I have to continually remind myself that were it not for television, I wouldn't be witnessing such incredible action.

Due to the thick coastal habitat of the Quinault Reservation land, there's much to be learned about bear behavior and overall population densities. While the spring hunts are when you'll find bears sporting their best, most luxurious coats, it's the fall hunts where you're likely to see the highest numbers of bears.

No doubt, the spring hunt will predictably hold the edge when it comes to scoring on a book skull, just because there are more big boars moving at this time. Also, during the month of April, these bears sport the finest quality, thickest, most coal-black pelts I've ever run my fingers through. For those hunters eager to attain a prime bear for a rug or lifesize mount, this is a fine place to look.

So, when is prime time hunt the Quinault? The sooner the better, as big bears become quickly educated. I'm fascinated by monster bears, so my number one choice would be late-April to mid-May, when bears are hitting baits with regularity. In the fall, as bears converge along the shores and tributaries of the world-renowned Quinault River to feast on migrating anadromous fish, double-digit bears on baits each evening can be the norm.

On one of my hunts at the Quinault, I explored a new area. We were less than 200 yards from the Pacific Ocean where the timber and vegetation was thick. The first night no bears hit the bait. On the second night, no sooner had I crawled into my treestand when the bears started coming in. Within an hour five bears would be beneath me.

Still, it wasn't the most bears I'd had roaming under my feet on the Quinault; that number stands at seven bears. But there was a good boar, one I wanted to take. As he approached the bait, I settled my BowTech into position.

The Gold Tip arrow passed clean through the thick-chested bear, then he was off. Moments later the coveted death moan rang out. Approaching the bear on hands and knees, through dense foliage that was too thick to walk upright in, the sound of the ocean waves crashing against the vertical rock cliffs below me made it tough hearing any activity in front of me.

One of my best bears on the Quinault, this one was taken from a treestand.

Fortunately, the big boar had expired on the trail, and another successful hunt on the Quinault had come to an end. With the taste of salt in the air and a cool breeze whisking through the trees, I couldn't have been more pleased. Right then and there I vowed to once again return to this great land, and I plan on holding myself to it.

Chapter 13:

Ground Blind Blacktail

Of all the big game I've been fortunate to hunt over the years, Columbia blacktail deer have taught me more than any other species. One of my most memorable hunts came from a ground blind, yielding one of my best bucks ever.

The trail cameras didn't lie. There were a couple big bucks that had moved in to the area, I just had to find them during daylight hours. I was hunting in one of my favorite blacktail settings–the foothills of Oregon's Cascades.

At this 1,500-foot elevation mark, there's a resident population of does as well as bucks. But when the rut kicks-in, bucks from higher elevations drop down in search of does in heat. The result is increased levels of competition among the bucks, and deer that can appear anywhere at any time.

It was late November, my favorite time to hunt this elevation. Though the peak of the rut has passed by this time, there are enough does around to keep lingering bucks interested, hoping to get some action in the second estrus cycle. This is a time when big bucks tend to cover more ground–like during the pre-rut, looking and sniffing for hot does.

Finding big blacktail bucks on trail cameras is one thing; locating them during shooting light is another. For the past few days two bucks in particular had been moving through one draw. Doe numbers were high in this drainage, both at the upper and lower elevations. The trail camera which had caught the two big bucks the most was situated at the upper elevations, near big timber and heavy brush.

Trail cameras are a blacktail hunter's best friend. This is the same buck I ended up arrowing about a week after the image was taken.

It only made sense that my hunting efforts should begin at the higher elevation. After two days and no sign of the big bucks, I left my treestand, grabbed a ground blind and headed to a lower elevation. My intent was to intercept the bucks as they moved between populations of does, rather than put all my eggs in one basket and hope they showed at the upper most site.

The next morning, ground blind in place, I hung a few urine drippers within bow range of the blind. I was situated at the base of a knoll, where two trails from two drainages converged. The purpose of the drippers, filled with doe urine, was to attract any bucks passing by.

Shortly after the first sign of light, two does crossed in front of me, 80 yards out. Behind them was a little buck, and behind him, a 160-inch monster 4x4. They continued down the ridge, out of sight.

Over the course of the next hour, amid a heavy fog and a slight drizzle, three bucks passed by the blind, one chasing does, the others sniffing the ground for any indications of a fertile female. None were what I considered to be shooters. Then, from the brush to my right, came a black-faced buck I'll never forget. He was a 3x4, but he was high, heavy and had good splits on both sides.

The obviously old buck never did follow the main trail, as is often the case with cagey, mature bucks. But he did check out two of my drippers, approaching each from different angles. When he stopped and sniffed the one at 15 yards, I did all within my power to keep from shooting him, hoping a bigger buck would appear. Had he carried an even 4x4 rack, he would have been pushing 150-inches, and no question been a shooter.

After a few sniffs, the buck walked off. I looked at my camera man, who just shook his head in denial. "What are you doing?" he scorned. "That was a giant buck!"

I knew exactly what he meant. "We have a few days, and I want that big buck," I replied.

An hour later, after having time to internalize my decision to pass that buck, I came to regret my choice. "If that 3x4 comes back, I'll take him," I shared with my camera man. He shot me a look that screamed, "Yeah, like that'll ever happen!"

Though I yearned to see the monster buck we'd caught glimpse of at first light, I knew I couldn't hold out for him should the 3x4 return. Big blacktails rarely offer a second chance.

Honestly, at this point, I still felt like we had a chance at both bucks. Where the blind was situated, the bucks had to pass by one side or the

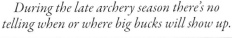

During the late archery season there's no telling when or where big bucks will show up.

113

other to get back to the thicker brush and big timber habitat they spend most of their time at in the hills above. The question was, would either pass by the blind on their return to higher ground.

As I sat pondering all the possibilities, replaying the motions the big 3x4 went through within spitting distance of me, I tried to not mentally give-in to the fact that no deer had to pass by the blind. It was big country, and the deer could go anywhere they pleased.

Suddenly, I was jolted back to reality. Not 75 yards in front of me came a half-dozen does, quickly feeding their way up the hill. The big 3x4 was right behind them.

Getting a second chance is something that rarely happens in the blacktail woods, especially with a bow and arrow. The closer the does came, the closer the buck came. Then, 40 yards in front of me, the does split apart. Because the buck was obscured by several small oak trees, I couldn't get a shot.

One group of does went to the right of the blind, just out of range, while the others went to the left side, in range but covered by brush. The buck followed the group to the left. Now, more than ever, I was regretting my bonehead mistake of passing him up. He was even bigger than I thought.

Dejected at what had just transpired, I felt helpless. Rummaging through my pack to find my doe bleat, the camera man tapped me on the shoulder and pointed out the left window. Here came our buck.

He wasn't happy with the does he'd followed, so was crossing over the base of the ridge to find the does that had disappeared into the timber to my right. In doing so, he moved right in front of us.

Confident he'd run right back under the nearest dripper, instead he peeled off and went on the other side of a stand of oak trees. No shot. Again, I felt my chances slipping away, for if he continued on that route, he'd soon be out of range.

Then he put his nose to the ground, lip-curled, turned 90° and started walking up the hill, right where I wanted him. Closer he drew with every step, and having already ranged several trees, I knew the distance.

When the buck cleared the last oak tree, I centered the bottom of my 20 yard pin on his chest, in the crease tight behind his front right leg. The BowTech Guardian got the arrow moving so fast, the buck didn't so much as flinch until the arrow had already blown through him.

Not passing up a second chance, I was more than happy to tag this handsome Columbia blacktail.

The blood trail left by the double-lung hit was easy to follow, and 40 yards from where I nailed him, I found my buck. I don't know what excited me most, the fact I'd just arrowed one of my best blacktails ever, or the fact I got a second chance at such a grand buck.

When it comes to blacktails, I find myself second-guessing my decisions more than with any other big game I pursue. They're an animal that forces you to think every moment of the hunt, draining you both mentally and physically.

On this hunt, however, everything worked out perfectly. The strategy to relocate paid off in the form of a record-book blacktail, and the fact I was able to pull it off from a ground blind, where encounters are intimate yet nerve-racking, only made the memories that much sweeter.

What made this hunt even more special was the fact we caught it all on film for the American Archer TV show, on the Outdoor Channel. Over the years, Tom Nelson, host of the American Archer, has allowed me to make several appearances on his show. Tom is one of the most sincere, most genuine men in the outdoor industry and I respect him

T.V. personality and noted archer, Tom Nelson–a man I greatly admire and respect–with an exceptional Oregon blacktail.

a great deal. Never one to boast about his accomplishments, Tom is a humble man who epitomizes what hunting and hunters are truly about. The bowhunting world needs more people like Tom Nelson.

When Tom began asking about a blacktail hunt for himself, in my home state, I was elated. In fact, he rolled in to town a few days after I took my 3x4 buck and hunted from the same blind I did.

I warned Tom how difficult these Columbia blacktails could be to hunt, and that it could take the better part of a week before he even saw a shooter buck. Less than an hour after crawling into the blind Tom had a dandy 4x4 walk right down the trail, following some does. A perfectly placed arrow launched from his BowTech did the job and soon Tom was admiring a record book blacktail most hunters only dream of.

I was elated for Tom and his great buck, but never heard the end of how "easy" these blacktails were compared to whitetails. That afternoon, Tom was on a plane back home to Michigan. In bowhunting, you take the easy ones when you can get them, and when it happens to be a big blacktail, it's that much sweeter; I'm sure Tom will come to realize that in future hunts to Oregon.

Chapter 14:

Land of the Big Bulls

Obviously, even when filming TV shows, not all hunts end in success. However, just because a tag goes unfilled doesn't mean the hunt was a bust. When it comes to chasing big bulls, this was one of my best hunts ever, and I never shot an arrow.

"You'll see a lot of big bulls, including some in the 380-inch range," shared Harold Gilchrist, owner of Landers Fork Outfitters in Great Falls, Montana. We were at a sportshow at the time, in Sacramento, California. We both had a booth at the show. Harold was selling guided deer and elk hunts, while my wife, Tiffany, and I were delivering seminars and selling books. But it was Tiffany's cooking that hooked Harold.

She was delivering multiple cooking seminars each day and she always had leftovers. The people in the booths around us were the first to get the delectable samples and Harold, seeing as how he was right next to us, was never left out.

Over the course of the five day show, I learned a lot about Harold and his hunting opportunities. By the end of the show we had scheduled an elk hunt for early September. Based on the stories Harold told me, the months couldn't pass fast enough.

I was the first hunter in camp and though we were early, felt we could get on some bulls. Harold had arrived a week earlier and built a couple natural ground blinds on the crest of some ridges, where he'd observed elk moving back and forth.

On the uphill hike during the first morning of our hunt, we heard a bull bugling ahead of us. We quietly stalked in for a closer look. The going was quiet in the moist, dew-laden grass, but we couldn't catch up with the fast-moving bull. Finally, 80 yards out, we caught a glimpse of him.

"What do you think he'll go?" I quizzed Harold. I already did some quick math, and figured the bull at 375-inches. When Harold came back with, "He'll be pushing 380," I knew I was in for a great week.

Though we never caught up with that bull, the standard had been set. Once I see big animals in an area, my downfall is I hate settling for anything less.

Admittedly, I was a bit frustrated. Bowhunting was new to Harold, and he didn't want me doing any calling for fear of educating the bulls. I tried talking him into it, but he was pretty set on not calling. This was only his second year of hunting this particular piece of ground, south of Great Falls, and he was still learning it. Prior to this, Harold spent more than 20 years in the backcountry, where rifle hunters made up nearly all of his clientele.

Finally, we made it into the blind where we sat the entire day. We didn't see a single elk. Though we heard a few bugling, I felt totally helpless. Pleading with Harold, I knew it was going to be a long week if I didn't put my calls to use.

"How about this, Harold," I asked. "You let me walk over the ridge, try a set of cow calls and if nothing answers, I'll quit bugging you about calling? But, if I get a reply, tomorrow we get to cover ground and keep calling."

At first he was hesitant, but my confidence in calling was getting the best of him. "You got a deal," he agreed.

Travis Ralls, my camera man on this hunt, and I headed over the hill and set up in a clump of young pine trees. Harold stayed on the ridge, watching. Knowing bulls weren't far, I let out a short, crisp cow mew. Immediately, four different bulls answered. Their bugles set off even more bulls, and just like that the valley was filled with sweet melodies.

One bull, no more than 100 yards away, came charging down through the timber, right in to our laps. He was a raghorn and we let him go right by. Minutes later another cow call brought a different bull our direction.

Over the course of the next 15 minutes there wasn't more than 30 seconds where a bugling bull couldn't be heard. Three bulls came to within 40 yards, but none were shooters, not after laying eyes on that 375-class brute.

JONH HINDERMAN PHOTO

When big bulls are bugling, it's hard to settle for anything less.

Once the bulls cleared we hiked back up to Harold who was watching everything from the ridge above. "That was incredible," he barked, still pumped with adrenaline. "That calling really does work, huh?" I just smiled.

"Tomorrow, let's get up here in the dark and you can start calling right away," Harold suggested. Travis and I looked at one another with joy in our eyes. Things were looking up.

The next morning we were back in our ground blind. My first cow calls got a bull bugling and there was no question he was moving up the hill in our direction. A few chirps followed by some high-pitched mews and the bull answered, but wouldn't budge. I tried stalking him but he had a harem of cows, thus too many eyes around to risk a stalk. I knew it was going to be tough pulling him away, but when the cows started coming to my calls, the bull followed.

One cow, hidden behind some thick brush, stood six yards from the blind. Then the bull crested the ridge, hit the edge of a meadow and walked within 20 yards of where we sat. "Shoot him, he's a good bull," Harold squeaked.

He was a nice 6x6, but no more than 300 inches. I wasn't about to put my tag on this guy knowing bigger bulls were around. After the bull took his harem into the timber, we hiked higher on the ridge and kept calling. Fresh rubs, a few wallows and the smell of rutting bulls left no doubt as to the number of elk in the area.

Working up a steep ridge, Harold kept his distance while Travis and I took the lead. Soon we found an ideal place to call. Letting loose with some excited cow chatter, three bulls responded; one from above, one from low to the left and another from across the canyon.

A hot mew enticed the bull across the canyon, who was soon barreling down a shale slope. It sounded like an avalanche as he busted through rock and scree. When he did reach the ridge we called from, the trees were too thick to see him, but there was no question as to what was happening.

In a matter of seconds we saw the bull's massive antlers dipping and twisting in an effort to negotiate the thick grove of young trees. It never ceases to amaze me, how fast and how easily these big animals can cover so much ground. When he stopped and bugled at 16 yards, I about lost it. He was all of 340-inches.

Anchored, camera rolling over my shoulder, all I needed was the bull to move a foot one way or another. A series of small trees blocked his vitals and no matter how hard I searched, I simply couldn't find a window to lace an arrow through. A minute passed and my bow felt heavy. Nearly two minutes into it I began to shake and knew I couldn't hold it much longer. That's when two cows popped out of the brush and the bull quickly turned and took off after them.

I wanted that bull in the worst way and was frustrated at having it be so close, yet not getting a shot. Just as I slid my arrow back into the quiver, Travis pointed up the hill. There, 60 yards away, was a 320-inch bull. He wasn't what we wanted, so we moved on.

We hadn't gone 30 yards when we bumped in to the third bull that had bugled. He was over 330-inches, so I tried calling him in so we could at least get some footage. No matter what I tried, he wouldn't leave his large harem. But another bull bugled a few ridges over.

Hoping for a bigger bull, we moved on. We called in a couple smaller bulls that evening, but nothing in the class we were looking for.

The next morning we were back at it, calling in a different section of land we'd not yet hunted. It was a great experience, for I was learning more about the land and how the elk lived within it, and Harold was learning about calling. It was a win-win situation, and we were having a blast.

Making our way to the point of a rocky outcropping we could see a herd of elk feeding on the edge of a small meadow, surrounded by timber. Below them was a dandy 4x4 mule deer. Down in the valley, through our spotting scope, we could see pronghorns, and not far from them, some whitetail deer.

A few minutes later, a black bear skirted the edge of a hill, rolling rocks and logs, looking for insects to feast on. Soon, a second bear followed. We searched high in the rocky cliffs above, and as amazing as it sounds, it was true. There stood three mountain goats, their white pelage leaving no question as to what they were.

From that one spot we could see six species of big game. Six! In all my years of hunting western big game, I'd never laid eyes on anything like it. Though the antelope and whitetails were too far away to get on film, Travis did capture all the other animals, and we talked about the experience while he was rolling tape. It's moments like this that make me thankful I'm a hunter, for without hunting, I'd not see such glorious sites.

Because there were so many bulls in the area we could be selective. We tried to first locate a big bull, then call to him. Finding what looked like a shooter bull, walking high in a clearing, he was over a half-mile

Natural springs flowing year-round keep bulls in this valley, along with exceptional feed and ample cover.

away. When I let out a call and he bugled, we knew we had a chance. But the closer we got to him, the more rugged the terrain became. At that point, we knew we'd have to try and call him to us.

He bugled at nearly every cow sound I made, but never moved our way. Then I started mixing in some simple bugles–nothing threatening, just enough to let him know another bull was treading on his turf. That got him moving.

It took a long time, nearly three hours, but finally we caught a glimpse of the bull. When we saw him approaching, alone, 70 yards out, we knew we had a chance. He went in to a little dip and we momentarily lost sight of him. When he came out of the trees, antlers covered in yellow grass he'd been thrashing, he let out an awesome bugle.

Travis and I both guessed him at close to 340-inches and worth taking. As the bull continued slowly striding our way, I reached full-draw. He moved through the sea of tall grass, but I needed him to get within 20 yards before his bulky chest cleared the high stocks of grass, giving me a shot. Two steps from where I wanted him, the bull turned, circled us and caught our wind. Just like that it was over.

One evening, Harold went to check out another ravine while Travis and I hiked to a new area. Right before dark we saw a massive, heavy-racked bull, alone, heading across a meadow. He was all of 350-inches but no matter how fast we moved, we couldn't catch him. He didn't so much as even acknowledge my cow calls.

The last point from which we called, Travis and I were in chest-deep, golden grass. We were surprised when another bull, one we hadn't seen, snuck up behind us. There we were, 50 yards from any brush and the bull walked within 20 yards of us. Sometimes elk do the craziest things; lucky for him he was a young bull.

Working toward some bigger timber, we had only enough time for one more setup. Glassing the hills from where we wanted to call, we spotted a giant bull bedded in some rocky terrain. I cow called and he bugled right back, still in his bed. Again I called and again he bugled.

Finally, he got up, stretched and bugled again. After spraying urine all over he turned and started trotting down the hill, right for us. He was still a good 600 yards out and with fading light, we knew he'd have to hurry. We had to stay in the open, for the timber was simply too dark to film in. The bull was a monster, pushing 380-inches. He could have been the first bull we saw on day one of the hunt but we weren't sure. We'd never find out, either, for we ran out of daylight before the bull reached us.

The next day we worked some upper ridgelines. One small bull came running in to the first setup. A raghorn came bugling into the second set. The third set produced a screaming bull, but he wouldn't budge.

Figuring he had cows he wasn't willing to leave, Travis and I stalked closer, calling as we went. Stopping about 75 yards from where we last heard the bull bugle, I let out a soft chirp. He answered right back. Another chirp, another bugle, but he wasn't moving. I got heavy in to some cow and calf talk, hoping the excited herd chatter would entice him–it didn't.

Taking a big, dead limb, I began scraping a pine tree in front of me. I followed it up with a single bugle. Cracking branches, shedding bark and kicking the ground to generate more noise, I hoped this aggressive challenge would do the trick. I bugled one more time, then cow called. Nothing.

"That worked good," I sarcastically remarked to Travis. Figuring the bull took his cows and split, I was about ready to get up and go when the bull appeared from nowhere, off to my extreme left. The 320-class bull came in silent, skirting around us to catch the wind. He stood broadside at 25 yards and was stunningly gorgeous in his dark mane and white-tipped headgear. But I felt we could do better and let the bull walk. Still, I learned a lot on that set, namely how aggressive hunters can be and how many tricks we can apply in an attempt to bring big bulls to within bow range. Sometimes I think we're too apprehensive, which costs us animals.

There were other close encounters along the way but either the bulls were too small or didn't offer a shot. On the last hour of the final day, Travis and I kicked in to high gear. I love running and gunning for elk–covering ground, cow calling, hearing a bugle then trying to quickly close-in.

We got two bulls fired-up. One came in, but wasn't a shooter. The other was answering every sound I made, but wasn't moving. Over the ridge, down the ravine and back up the next ridge we went. We were getting closer, but still the bull wasn't budging.

As we entered the dark timber Travis shot me a nod. "It's awful low light in here," he pointed out. My absolute favorite time to hunt elk is the last hour of the day. This is when bulls are active and more approachable than any other time. The frustrating part, the later it gets, the worse the filming conditions become and entering into dark timber doesn't help matters.

When in timber we might lose our filming light 20 to 30 minutes sooner than we would by remaining in the open. It's frustrating, for that's some of the best habitat to approach bulls in. I think it's situations like this that explain why my hairline is receding so rapidly.

Under these circumstances, on the final day, we had no choice. Light was fading fast and the bull wasn't budging. We had to go to him. Travis ditched the 30-pound tripod and we took off on a run. A couple hundred yards into the trees we stopped and called. The bull answered, still in the same place. I called a few more times–hyper cow sounds all the way–and still he didn't seem to be moving.

Letting out an aggressive bugle didn't work. Nor did raking the trees. Again he answered my cow sounds, but wouldn't move.

"You have 10 minutes," Travis instructed.

Quickly moving through the trees we cut the distance in half. I called and the bull answered, no more than 50 yards away. His raspy, powerful bugle is a sound I'll never forget. The way it overpowered the calm woods was almost intimidating and resoundingly eerie in the waning light.

I could see a rise in the land on the other side of which was a ravine. Figuring the bull had a wallow in there, I inched forward. I called again, and again he bugled back. He hadn't moved.

Now I was within 40 yards of the bull, but had yet to lay eyes on him.

"Two minutes," whispered Travis.

Though I called in many bulls on this trip, I never shot an arrow. Still, it was one of the best elk hunts of my life and I learned a lot.

Desperately I called but the bull quit answering. Again I gave him an excited cow mew but the woods remained silent. Knowing the hunt was almost over I figured the bull caught on to us and headed up the draw.

Just as I grabbed my bow and broke into the open, hoping to catch the bull moving in the bottom of the ravine, here he came, stepping over the rise that had separated us. Busted! But in such low light conditions, you never know how a bull will react. As long as he didn't wind us, I still thought I had a chance.

Steady as stones Travis and I crouched, unable to move for fear of spooking the bull. Inside 30 yards, the mountain monarch held firm, staring right at us. His high, black rack with its long, ivory points, was largely obscured by small trees. Because he was facing me, I couldn't tell how long the tines were, but there was no question he carried a giant main frame.

"It's now or never!" Travis whispered.

Situating a diaphragm call in my mouth, I came to full-draw while simultaneously rocking to my knees. The bull got nervous and I cow called. There were simply too many trees to chance a shot on a moving bull. He never did stop.

"How big was he?" I asked Travis, plucking the arrow from the string.

"You don't want to know," he replied, powering down the camera.

I never ran the footage back to take a look at that bull. I didn't want to. I was content with the magnificent image etched in my mind's-eye, which is always bigger than what the camera reveals. I guessed him at 360-inches, but it was hard to tell for sure as so many trees stood between us.

All I know it was a fitting end to one of the most incredible hunts of my life. In all, we called in 18 bulls to within bow range and caught all of them on film. It's experiences like this where hunters learn so much. During that hunt I made more than my share of mistakes, but came away a better hunter because of it.

On the flight back home I thought, "What if I had taken one of the first bulls I saw earlier in the hunt?" Then I wouldn't have been able to call in so many other bulls nor observe some true giants and how they behave in specific situations.

Though I didn't shoot an arrow that trip, I consider it one of my most successful hunts, ever. What I learned was invaluable and surpassed what I'd experienced in many entire seasons spent in the woods. Where else can we learn so much in such a short period of time than when we're actually amongst the animals we pursue?

Experiences like this make me realize how fortunate we truly are to live in a country where we can hunt. Having traveled and hunted in many exotic locales, I can say from first-hand experience, we really are blessed with the opportunities we have in America, where hunting elk tops the list for so many sportsmen.

Chapter 15:

Spot & Stalk Antelope

Warm weather, easy terrain and good friends make pronghorn hunting a favorite among many people. Having plenty of animals to look at, and the fact a Pope & Young buck can pop-up just about anywhere, also adds to the joy of these hunts.

In my job as a TV host, the toughest duties are carried-out by the camera man. I've worked with many camera crews over the years, some good, some not so good. The ones who struggled didn't last long. The ones who were good are still around. The exceptional ones make their sole living running cameras while others do it as a part time job.

One of the best camera men I worked with was Bret Stuart. Bret is from my hometown of Springfield, Oregon. We even attended the same high school. Bret and I met on the river one summer, where he worked as a salmon and steelhead guide. These same duties would later take him away from being my videographer. We shared many fond memories together on the river, and during those years we had no idea that we'd soon spend three years together filming TV shows.

When I served as host of various titles on the Men's Channel, including BowTech's Western Adventures, Bret was my camera man. He also filmed several hunts of appearances I made on Outdoor American and American Archer. He is an accomplished hunter, knows the outdoors well and is a hard-working man. He was also one of the best off-hand videographers I've ever seen.

Videographers put in long days, longer than the host. They're awake before everyone, readying cameras and gear. They have more buttons to push and controls to monitor on their equipment than I do shooting a bow. At the end of the day, they log, download and backup footage, hitting the sack well after everyone else has turned-in for the night.

Because of their hard work and passion for the outdoors, I like seeing my camera men hunting when the opportunity arises. Switching roles–putting them in front of the camera and me behind it–makes me fully appreciate how hard their job really is.

On this hunt, Bret and I were with Reese Clarkson of Mill Iron Outfitters in South Dakota. By this time we'd filmed several hunts with Reese. When I connect with someone like Reese, whom I truly love being around, I like returning as often as possible. My main purpose is to share with the rest of the hunting world what great people there are in our fraternity and how good the hunting can be.

Bret had always wanted to hunt pronghorns and now his dream was coming true. BowTech Tribute dialed in, Bret wanted to do it spot-and-stalk and this was the place to pull it off. The first few stalks went awry for various reasons. Stalking antelope in short grass, with many eyes upon you, isn't easy. The fact the rut was slow in developing didn't help things.

Finally, we found a lone buck laying scrapes every 50 or so yards, stopping to rub his facial glands on about every piece of sage brush in between. The good part, the buck was moving straight away from us. The bad part, the vegetation was sparse, meaning there was virtually no cover to assist in a stalk.

The first 200 yards went easy, then it got tough. Rather than risk my spooking the animal with the big camera and giant tripod, I stayed back the final 100 yards. Filming the stalk from a distance is one of my favorite ways to shoot a TV show, for it accurately puts into perspective exactly what's happening. Getting the hunter and the animal in frame at the same time, I believe, makes for some of the most real television possible. It's a true portrayal of what hunting out West is all about, especially when it comes to spot-and-stalk action.

Bret played the stalk perfectly. Every time the buck would drop his head, Bret moved forward. When the buck would pick up speed and walk straight away, Bret would almost break into a run. It took several minutes but it was working.

Whenever the buck stopped and looked around, Bret would hunker down and hold perfectly steady. Bret drew closer with every step, then I saw him reach for the rangefinder for the first time. From my perspective, straight behind Bret, it looked like he was within 30 yards of the buck. I was dumbfounded, for how he pulled off a seemingly impossible stalk in such open terrain was beyond me.

Nocking and arrow and reaching full-draw, Bret's movement caught the buck's attention. For the first time in over 300 yards of stalking, the buck saw Bret. I think Bret was so close, the buck couldn't figure out what was happening. Wasting no time, however, Bret let his Gold Tip arrow fly and it found the mark.

Bret Stuart made an incredible shot on this spot-and-stalk antelope. Bret was one of the hardest working camera men I had the honor of working with.

The buck went a short distance and died on its feet, tumbling through dirt and sage. When Bret told Reese and I the shot came at 67 yards, we were surprised. Bret's shooting didn't shock us, as he's an excellent shot with the bow. What did surprise us was how close he looked to the animal from our perspective. All came together perfectly and Bret was happy to wrap his fingers around the horns of his first pronghorn.

On the same hunt, I'd pull-off one of my most memorable big game stalks of all time. It was the first morning, only minutes into the hunt, and we watched a buck separate from the herd. While does and younger bucks moved into a sage-covered draw to bed, the buck went on to a grassy flat and laid down.

He was nearly a mile away and through the spotting scope we could see he wasn't a monster buck. But the fact he was alone, in a stalkable position, I decided to try for him.

Wasting no time, Bret and I closed the first 1,200 yards in quick fashion, as we were out of sight from the buck. Reese stayed back to watch the stalk from afar. The last few hundred yards weren't as simple, as now the buck was in full-view.

For the final 150 yards I slipped off my boots while Bret stayed back with the camera set on the tall tripod. Again, he'd be able to capture the action on film with both the hunter and the target animal in full-frame.

Fortunately, there weren't any cacti on this piece of ground, only hard dirt and short, golden grass. It was late August and the sun-parched land made being quiet a major challenge. The wind was lightly drifting sideways from right to left. The buck was bedded in the grass, broadside to my position, his head facing straight away.

Because the grass was only a few inches tall my goal was to keep the buck's head facing straight away from me at all times. Every step I took, I keyed on the back of the buck's head. The way an antelope's eyes are set high and to the outside of the skull means their field of view is vast. I knew if the buck so much as turned his head, I'd get busted.

Fearing the buck would turn his head at some point, I moved faster than I normally would have, but I didn't want to go too slowly and get busted.

Before I knew it I was inside 50 yards and at the point from which I'd hoped to take a shot. Unfortunately, the buck was bedded on the backside of a tiny burm which covered his vitals. I had no choice but to move closer.

Though not a big buck, the stalk I pulled-off on this pronghorn was the most memorable of my bowhunting career.

At 40 yards his vitals were still covered. At 30 yards I was seeing more of what I wanted but it still wasn't enough for a shot. Palms sweaty, I just knew I was going to get busted. My last range on the buck read 24 yards. Tiptoeing ever so gently on the hardpan ground, I covered three more yards.

Finally, after a lengthy stalk I was 21 yards from the buck that we'd first seen from a mile out. Anchoring the BowTech, I thought for certain he'd catch my movement. When I touched the release, the arrow buried behind his right front shoulder and immediately I felt a wave of relief flow through my body.

The buck was far from the biggest we'd seen on the trip, in fact, he was barely average, but that didn't matter. On this hunt, Bret and I pulled off what seemed like two impossible stalks on what many archers consider to be the toughest animal to stalk in North America. Of all the TV episodes I've shot to this point in my career, this is still one of my all-time favorites.

A couple seasons later I'd be back with Reese, this time filming a hunt for my Game Chaser TV show. This time the bucks were rutting and we wanted to pull-off the hunt with the use of a decoy.

Scott Koan, Reese's top guide, is a man I'll hunt with any time, anywhere, for anything. He's very tuned-in to animals and their behavior and knows how to read and wisely use the land to his advantage. I've shared some of my most memorable muley and antelope bowhunting moments with Scott. This trip would be no different.

We were in to the third day of a five day hunt and each day we had multiple stalks. I could have shot over a half-dozen bucks via spot-and-stalk, but wanted to bring a buck to the decoy. Finally, we caught a break.

From high atop a hillside we could see three bucks chasing a single doe in the bottom. It was obvious she was in heat, and the bucks were chasing each other, hard, then prodding the doe. They were moving into the head-end of a small ravine, and using the cut-banks and gumbo ridges we felt we could get close.

During the course of the stalk we lost sight of the bucks for over 10 minutes. When we came up to the backside of an eroded island in the middle of a washed-out drainage, they were nowhere to be seen. We searched, but couldn't find them.

"They either moved out of here or they're very close, on the

Pronghorns are one of my favorite species to pursue. The weather is usually warm and there are plenty of animals, offering the perfect learning situation for archers.

backside of this island," whispered Scott. Suddenly, Reese, who stands taller than Scott and I, crouched down. "They're right over this island, inside 50 yards and heading our way," Reese shared.

Reese and Scott stayed put, while I crawled around the right side of the island and moved slightly ahead. The height of the cut bank was about six-feet, offering the perfect concealment to get me in shooting position. If the antelope continued on the same path Reese had last seen them, they'd pass within 10 yards of where I sat.

After what seemed an eternity, but in actuality was only a few minutes, the doe finally appeared. She didn't stay in the bottom of the wash like I'd hoped, rather popped up on to the far bank of the dry creekbed. She didn't see us, and slowly fed her way along the sage, 20 yards from me.

Glancing back at Reese and Scott, they confirmed the buck was following the doe. All I had to do was wait. Then the doe lifted her head and stared right at me. I was busted, in the wide open, and didn't so much as blink. At that moment, Scott slowly lifted the decoy. The instant he made that move, the doe lifted her head and took a few strides forward. The buck followed.

As soon as the buck cleared the gumbo knob, I swung into position. This shot was taken a few seconds before I released the arrow.

Teamwork is what allowed me to take this South Dakota pronghorn.

The buck hadn't yet seen the decoy, as he was focused on the doe. Where the other two bucks went, I didn't know and didn't care. I knew the shooting window was going to close quick and told myself I'd take any of the three bucks that gave me the chance.

Just as the buck slipped into my view he turned and saw the decoy. Scott and Reese had the decoy 10 yards behind me and a few yards off to my left. With the buck moving from left to right in front of me, and his attention turned toward the decoy, I caught a millisecond of time at which to reach full-draw.

At 20 yards, my BowTech Admiral, shooting right at 300 feet-per-second, shoved the Gold Tip arrow clean through the buck. He sprinted 70 yards, stopped, staggered and tipped over.

Hunts like this are something I never tire of. Though the pressure of capturing them for television is sometimes more stressful than I'd like, when it comes to pronghorns there's just a different feeling in the air. Warm summer days, lots of animals to look over, easy terrain to negotiate and good friends, make for some of my favorite, most memorable hunts the West has to offer.

Chapter 16:

Subzero Mule Deer

Late season mule deer hunts offer some of the best opportunities for archers to score on a record-class buck. Then again, the conditions can be brutally cold, impacting deer movement, their behavior and how you go about hunting them. Fortunately, all things came together on this bone-chilling hunt.

A quick look around the vast land left us a bit concerned. In a place normally crammed full of mule deer this time of year, we saw only a few head. A major storm had blasted through this portion of South Dakota two days prior and many deer were gone. How far they went was anyone's guess and given the labyrinth of cuts, draws, gullies and ravines to hide in, there was no telling for sure where they were.

The next morning found us atop a knoll, greeting a stunning sunrise in minus 13° temperatures. Through the spotting scope we'd find some mule deer, their white, frost-covered backs glistening in the growing light. But no good bucks were to be found. We moved on.

The next high point found us looking into a timbered draw, one where Reese Clarkson had seen a high-racked 4x4 buck a few days earlier. "The last time I saw him he was with nine does, right on that hillside," pointed Clarkson. "Given the bad weather we've had, I bet he held tight in the tree belt. He won't be far."

By this time I'd had many great hunts with Clarkson, and was learning more about the land and deer that lived there. Twenty-four hours earlier I'd wrapped-up a rifle hunt for whitetails in the northeast corner of Wyoming. Today, I was intent on trying to fill a South Dakota mule deer tag which would give me two deer in two states with two

Though peak rut is over, late November and December is a great time to get after South Dakota's mule deer. There always seems to be a buck chasing does around.

different hunting approaches in two days. Both hunts were caught on film for Outdoor America, a show I used to cohost on the Outdoor Channel.

As we continued glassing the trees and connecting ravines, I couldn't help but reflect on the many exciting hunts Reese and I had shared together on his place over the past few seasons. A year earlier, on Halloween, I stalked to within 17 yards of a 29-inch wide 4-point buck and slipped an arrow into his lungs. Before that I took my biggest pronghorn to date, with a rifle, and another record book buck with a bow. The animals are there and the best part if you're a nonresident archer, the tags are guaranteed.

By simply applying on-line a nonresident bowhunter can purchase a deer or antelope tag any time of the season, right up to the end. It's a great way to extend your hunting season, especially if you weren't lucky in drawing tags from other western states.

"There he is," whispered Reese, snapping me out of a daze. I was so deep in thought, I failed to notice the cold slime trail running from my nose to my upper lip. My jaw muscles were tight from the freeze, making it hard to talk. Thankfully no words were needed, for I picked up on the buck as he moved out of the bottom of a draw, complete with nine does.

"As soon as they drop into that next draw, you can make your move," encouraged Reese. Soon they were out of sight and I was on my way. Only a skiff of snow covered the ground but it was frozen solid and made for noisy going in the still, crisp air. Just as I got ready to plunge into the draw in hopes of finding taller grass to muffle my sound, the herd emerged on the opposite hillside, less than 100 yards away. It was there they bedded with the morning sun hitting them square-on. The buck was in the middle and with so many eyes around him there was no chance of getting within range, not this time.

We backed out and drove to new ground, hoping to find another buck to stalk. Six hours later and no shooter bucks found, we returned to where we'd seen the buck at first light. Not 200 yards from where we last saw him, there was our buck. This time, however, the situation was in our favor.

The buck was bedded next to a single doe, the rest of the herd spread amid the tree belt and adjacent hillsides, feeding. With the rut still on his mind, the buck was focused on one doe. Playing the wind, we figured I could slip into a creek bottom, up the backside of the knoll he was bedded on, and maybe, just maybe, get to within bow range.

Hunting in the sub-zero temperatures reminded
me of my subsistence living days in Alaska's Arctic region.

The second I set foot in the bottom of the gully, I told myself it wasn't going to happen. I tried remaining positive but it just didn't feel right. The snow and leaves were so crunchy, so noisy, there was little doubt the deer would hear me. But I pushed on, reminding myself that the buck was rut-crazed.

Continuing slowly and as quietly as possible, I found myself beneath the tree I'd marked to be in direct line with the bedded deer. I was within 80 yards of the buck, if he was still there. The crest of a knoll stood between us and there was only one option awaiting me: walk straight at him.

Three steps closer and two deer spooked out of the trees below me. They ran out in front and I was sure they'd alert the buck. But not knowing for sure, I continued inching forward. Five minutes later, still battling crunchy snow, I could see the two deer I'd jumped, standing on the opposing hillside, looking back at me.

Tediously picking my way forward, I soon saw the tips of the big buck's rack. He was still bedded in the same spot. A few more yards and the doe's ears stood out. Given his position, there was no shot opportunity and I had no choice but to wait for him to stand.

Darkness would soon be upon us and the now 8° temperatures combined with a breeze took the windchill to well below zero. The question now was, "Who would give-in first?" Would the deer stand, or would my fingers chill to the point of not being able to maintain bow control?

Minutes passed, then the doe quickly stood, alert. It was obvious something spooked her. She'd been watching the two does I'd scared earlier and sent across to the opposing hillside. She grew nervous, stood, and started prancing right for me, away from where she thought the source of danger to be. She had no idea I was there, and as soon as she moved, so did the buck,

At 12 yards she saw me, but I remained still, trying to keep her from sprinting off. The buck got to within 20 yards, and I quickly came to full-draw, hoping he'd turn. I repeatedly grunted but nothing stopped him. He was focused on the doe and nothing was going to change that.

He stuck to her tail, dropped out of sight behind some sage and emerged just over 50 yards out. The doe finally stopped and looked back, giving me the chance to hit her with the range finder. Getting two firm readings just beyond 60 yards, I felt confident about taking the shot. Fortunately, the buck stopped right behind her and I knew his exact distance.

Bringing my BowTech Guardian to full-draw, the cold temperatures were not even felt. Slight pressure on my release sent the arrow on it's way and into the lower chest of the buck. The recovery was quick.

Taken in temperatures below zero, I couldn't have been happier with this high-racked buck.

It was now 8° below zero°–colder than that with the windchill–as the sun plunged beneath the horizon. On outings like this, the harsh conditions only add to the memories of the hunt. It took me back to the days I lived and hunted in the Alaskan Arctic, where snow covered the ground nine months of the year, and below zero temperatures were the norm for more than 200 days.

On this hunt I reaffirmed the value of being a patient bowhunter. Had I pushed the stalk the first time I saw this buck, at first light, I would have likely educated him, making it tougher for me to close the deal later on. Worse yet, I could have pushed him out of the country and never seen him again. In the end, patience and persistence paid-off, and I couldn't have been more pleased sticking my tag on this high-racked, December mule deer.

Chapter 17:

Second Chance Blacktail

Over the past decade, the popularity of hunting from treestands has grown considerably in the blacktail community. The amount of wildlife you see while sitting in a stand can be nothing short of incredible, but the best part, you get to watch how animals behave, naturally, without them even knowing you're there.

As anticipated, a small three-point walked down the trail, right under my treestand. He wasn't a shooter but the one following him was close. The trailing buck was also a three-point, pushing 18-inches wide. He was an older deer, sporting heavy bases and long tines, but he wasn't the buck I was hoping for.

During mid-summer scouting missions I'd seen these bucks, and one other, living in the area. A few days prior to the September opener, I saw all three bucks together. At that time they were in velvet; now it had all been stripped away.

Holding out for the biggest of the three bucks, after an hour of waiting, I knew it wasn't going to happen. "He should have been here by now," I thought to myself, perched 23-feet up in a tree. The three bucks had been traveling together since July, and nothing had changed, other than their velvet being shed.

The buck I wanted was a tall, heavy-racked brute, at least two years older than the others. "Maybe he already went nocturnal," I pondered. After all, he was the oldest of the trio.

It just didn't make sense. We were only a couple days into the season and his patterns shouldn't have changed that much. I surmised that either the older buck went to be alone, as big bucks

I could have shot this buck beneath my treestand numerous times during the late August season opener, but was holding out for his bigger counterpart.

often do this time of year, or there was an intruder in my hunting area.

The following day I found the buck, dead. A cougar had killed him 75 yards from my treestand. As if trophy blacktails aren't hard enough to tag, toss a predator into the equation and the challenge rises rapidly.

Right then and there I made the decision to pack it up and return during the late season, in November. I was hunting the foothills of Oregon's Cascade Range in an area where I'd taken bucks before. There weren't as many resident deer around this year, now I knew why. Nothing will drive big blacktail bucks from their core area faster than a cougar.

My hopes were that by the November season the cougar would be gone and more bucks would move down from the hills in search of does. My plan paid-off.

A couple days before Thanksgiving I was back in the same spot. By this time more deer had moved in and there was no sign of the big cat.

Most of the bucks passing beneath and around my stand were smaller than what I'd hoped for, so I waited. Then, in the middle of the afternoon, a mature buck weaseled his way out of the forest, following a single doe. It was obvious she was in heat as he was going everywhere she went.

When she stopped, he stopped. When she moved, he moved. Down the hill they went, out of range, disappearing into a deep, wooded ravine. A few minutes later they popped out of the green curtain of Douglas fir trees, 60 yards in front of me. The doe headed right for the trail on which I sat.

"I'm on him, so shoot when you want," whispered Travis Ralls, my camera man. When I told him the buck was too small, he shot me a look I'd seen all too often. People often remark on my taking a good number of big animals and wonder how I do it. Really, it's simple. Work hard, never quit and don't shoot the small ones.

True, it was a big, mature four-point, and I probably should have looked at him a bit closer. But he was a tad spindly and had broken off part of the his right G4. Not that the broken tine mattered, I just thought I could do better. Besides, we had three days to hunt and I didn't want to take the first good buck we laid eyes on.

The buck followed the doe as she slowed down and fed, 20 yards from our stand. We watched that buck for over 10 minutes. Had I shot him, the hunt would have been over in less than 30 minutes. As it was, we got to observe his natural behavior during the peak of the rut. That's something not many people get the opportunity to enjoy as they usually try killing the deer by that point.

It was amazing to see how aggressive he was toward not only the doe, but smaller bucks as well. Anytime a buck came close, he chased it off. When his doe moved, he got right back by her side, or should I say tail. When she urinated, he sniffed it to sense what her estrogen levels registered.

One time she got so tired of being pestered and prodded, she laid down in the middle of the shortest grass around. She didn't seem to care about taking cover, she was just flat-out tired of being chased. The buck never left. The second she stood, there he was, sniffing her backside.

I was so enamored in watching this buck's behavior, I totally dismissed the possibility of shooting him. When the buck followed the doe up the hill, into and old stand of fir trees, I turned and smiled at Travis. We agreed that what we'd just witnessed was special and it was even more thrilling to know Travis got all the action on film for our Game Chasers show. I also snapped several still photos of the buck.

My camera man wasn't happy when I passed this buck. A few days later he came back by our stand.

"Why didn't you shoot him," Travis questioned.

"We have time," I smiled.

That afternoon, no more bucks came by the stand. We didn't see anything the next day, either. Now, with time running out, I asked myself the same thing, "Why didn't I shoot him?"

We did see a big four point on the third day, but he never came within range. He was bigger than the buck I passed, but never left the doe he was with. I would have shot that buck in a second but never had the opportunity.

A week prior to my hunting this piece of ground, fellow TV host and renowned bowhunter, Tom Miranda, arrowed a monster blacktail from the same stand I'd been hunting from. Tom was on a quest for his North American big game slam with his bow, and after seven days of hunting, finally got his first shot at a blacktail. After filling his tag–and with only three more animals to go on his slam–Tom commented that the Columbia blacktail was the toughest animal to attain thus far. That brought a smile to all the blacktail fanatics around.

Tom Miranda put in some serious days of hunting before tagging this giant Columbia blacktail in southern Oregon. He shot it from the exact treestand I later arrowed my buck from.

The next day was Thanksgiving and Travis and I drove home to spend it with my family. The following morning we were back in the stand, greeted by a heavy fog.

Fog is good for hunting, bad for filming. We had a good size forked-horn move through, and a smaller three-point, neither of which were shooters. Even if they had been worth taking, I couldn't have shot, for the fog was too thick, not allowing our high definition camera to do it's job.

It took until late morning for the fog to lift and we committed to sitting in the stand all day long. One mistake I see hunters making this time of year is leaving their stands in the middle of the day. When the rut is on and bucks are constantly on the move, you never know when a big one might pass by.

Furthermore, it was a full moon. On full moons I like hunting all day long, especially during the rut. The reason is, does still have to feed, preparing their bodies for the upcoming winter. They know they'll have a developing fetus or two to also sustain through the toughest months of the year and can't afford to let their bodies get run-down.

December, January and February are the hardest months on a blacktail's body. Though they have plenty of food to eat, it has virtually no nutritional value at this time. In fact, it's possible for deer to die with full stomachs, having actually starved to death due to the lack of nutrition in what they're eating. Biologists have proven this time after time.

Does do most of their feeding at night, but on full moon nights, during the rut, often get chased so aggressively by bucks, they aren't able to get their fill. The does get so flustered at being chased, they bed down early. By mid-day they often get hungry and start feeding. If a doe is in heat you can bet a buck won't be far.

Once the fog lifted we could see much better and it was obvious deer were active. On the opposite hillside a small buck chased a doe. Beneath us the forked-horn that came by earlier that morning, passed by again. This time Travis got him on film.

Other, smaller bucks were crossing the knoll on which we sat, looking to score on any doe that might be in heat. Twice, two young bucks paused to spar. It wasn't an all-out fight, but was fun to watch, nonetheless.

Then, suddenly, both Travis and I heard it at the same time. Thundering footsteps of a running deer. The air was dead-calm, and the ground, heavy with dew from the thick fog which blanketed it most of the morning.

Thud...Thud...Thud! It was closing-in fast. We hadn't even seen it, but both reacted at the same instant. I quickly plucked my bow from the holder while Travis turned on the camera and started rolling tape.

At the instant we were ready, a big buck came into view. The doe he chased down the hill was silently galloping, but the buck pounded the ground hard with each leap.

"He's a shooter," I whispered to Travis.

"But he's the broken tined four point," he replied.

I don't know if it was the adrenaline rush I felt from hearing the buck's fast, aggressive approach, or what, but to me he looked much larger than when we'd seen him a few days prior. Sure enough, a closer look confirmed he was the same buck.

Travis is the hardest working camera man I've ever worked with. He has incredible eyes, way better than mine, and though I wasn't doubting him I really was hoping it was a different buck. Over the years Travis and I have shared the most memorable hunts of my life. We have TV to thank for bringing us together and for allowing us to live our dreams of making a living through the outdoors. We have the best jobs on the planet and we both know it and thank the good Lord for it each and every day.

"What do you think?" I quizzed Travis, always respectful of his input.

"Shoot him!" was all he replied, never taking his eye off the camera.

I'd already taken ranges of all the trees and stumps within a 50 yard radius, so when the buck broke the 40 yard barrier, I knew it was time to get serious. This time, the doe he was chasing came even closer to our stand. When she jumped over the log that lay 15 yards away, and stopped, I anchored the kisser button in the corner of my mouth.

My body was still shaking from the quickened pace at which the buck approached, and I desperately tried to stay calm. I remember being surprised at how easy my 72 pound BowTech Admiral drew–adrenaline and frail nerves will have that affect.

When I put my top pin where I wanted it, I was shocked at how steady it seamed. Almost by itself the bow sent the arrow, driving it through the buck and into the ground on the opposite side.

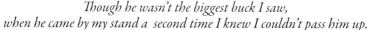

Though he wasn't the biggest buck I saw,
when he came by my stand a second time I knew I couldn't pass him up.

In the Haugen family, blacktails are a year-round passion.

The buck kicked his hind legs, ran a short distance then slowed down. His blood loss was immense. He didn't go far.

The fact I got a second chance on that buck–a buck we saw on day one of this hunt–convinced me it was meant to be. He was a nice buck, making the record book by a good margin, but that's not what mattered. What mattered was that we cleanly took a mature blacktail on a very memorable hunt, and in my book, any blacktail you take with a bow is an accomplishment to be proud of.

As Travis and I dragged the buck down a logging road, toward the truck, something simultaneously caught our eyes. Not 200 yards from our treestand, fresh cougar tracks were in the middle of the wet, muddy road. How fresh were they? They were in our boot prints we'd made that morning while hiking in to our stand. That was all the confirmation I needed to know I'd made the right choice in tagging this buck. Some things are just meant to be.

Chapter 18:

Wyoming Elk Quest

My first bowhunt in Wyoming's rugged wilderness yielded the most memorable elk hunt of my life. Could the following year offer a repeat performance?

On September 1, 2003, good friends, Bob Wells, Tom Buller, and I filled our tags on three record book bulls in Wyoming's Absaroka Range. Fortunately, the following year, I once again drew the coveted tag.

With the drawing held early in the year, I had plenty of time to imagine how our upcoming hunt might play out. But the biggest question in my mind, "Was the previous year's experience a fluke, or would the bulls be in there again?"

We were 22 miles back into the Wyoming wilderness–18 by horse, four on foot. When hunting a designated wilderness area in Wyoming, nonresidents are required to either have a guide or be accompanied by a resident who registers with the game and fish department, which Bob did for me this time around.

We were hunting a big burn that swept through the area in the late '90s. On a north facing slope, a large patch of timber escaped the flames, and that's where we took our bulls a year earlier. Days could be spent hunting that timber stand, which was rich in food, offered prime cover and had clear-flowing creeks in every draw. In such ideal elk habitat, and given the fact we observed rubs and wallows that had been made over the course of the past several years, we felt our chances of success were high.

The timber patch we hunted was situated just below the 10,000 foot level and getting there was physically excruciating. The four mile hike from base camp into the hunting area required a good three hours due

Our first do-it-yourself journey into Wyoming's backcountry made for the best elk hunt of my life.

to the ruggedness of the terrain. The going was also delayed due to all the blown down trees we had to negotiate.

At times we walked 50 yards atop blackened logs without ever touching the ground. Each winter an increasing number of burned trees got blown down, and I honestly don't know how much longer we'd be able to hunt the area. Several layers of trees stacked atop one another often found us 15 feet off the ground, and in the back country, so far from medical attention, one missed step could have turned the hunt into a life-threatening ordeal.

On the trail in, Tom's horse went berserk, kicked, bucked and sprinted by the packstring before slamming Tom to the ground. Had Tom not broken his fall into a boulder patch, the situation could have been much worse than just a sore, scraped jaw and bruised arms.

The moment Tom got bucked off, his horse went barreling down a steep hill, hurdling and busting through blow downs at breakneck speed. The power and quickness of the horse was mind boggling. After a quarter-mile sprint the horse buckled beneath a jumble of blown-down trees, landing tight against a stack of upended root wads.

Though I wanted to bury him right there, we were actually fortunate that the once wild horse emerged with little more than a few scratches. The saddle and loaded bags ended up under his belly. A front foot was thrust through a stirrup and Tom's bow had been demolished.

Leading your own packstring into the rugged backcountry can be the most dangerous part of a do-it-yourself hunt. Such wrecks make those guided hunts and the wranglers who are so proficient at handling horses, that much more appreciated.

Later that afternoon we finally arrived in camp. We had no time to scout, and scrambled to set up the tent, get the horses fed, devour some MREs and hit the sack. Sleep didn't come easy, for just like the previous year, elk bugled all around us.

The next morning, Tom, without a bow to hunt with, stuck close to camp to man the horses. Bob and I hiked down into the hole, heading for the big, timbered ridge. A mile from camp we came to the edge of the giant canyon and sat back to take in the beauty of the land as darkness gave way to daylight. A few elk bugled throughout the valley below, as did a pair on the hillside on which we sat.

Working down the slope, a good sounding bull let out a bugle right around the corner. Bob responded with a cow call and the bull fired right back. So aggressive was the bull, we could hear brush cracking as his repetitive bugles echoed throughout the valley.

At 90 yards the six-point stood in an open stretch of green grass, bugling amid the lifeless timber surrounding him. Minutes slowly passed until a change in the wind sent him barreling to safety.

Continuing to the bottom of the canyon and up the other side, Bob and I finally arrived in the lush timber we knew held many elk. To our surprise the first calling setup didn't elicit a bugle. Moving 200 yards to the west, into the next creek bottom, fresh droppings, rubs and a well used wallow left no doubt a bull was in the area.

Setting up again, Bob let loose with a hyper cow call and I followed with a few calf sounds. Immediately a bull fired back, and within seconds his wide rack could be seen swaying through the trees. For the first 75 yards he came without hesitation. At 60 yards he paused behind a tree and spent several minutes searching. Bob and I teamed up on some subtle cow calls, finally convincing the bull to move forward.

At 40 yards the bull walked through an opening and Bob stopped him with a quick call. Unfortunately, Bob's arrow flew over the bull's back and he sprinted off. But in the world of rut-crazed bulls, it's never over. Immediately, Bob cut loose with some loud, aggressive cow mews. Instantly the bull stopped behind some thick brush. A few more calls brought the bull circling back in and this time Bob's 32 yard shot found the mark.

The bull dashed off and toppled less than 50 steps from where he was hit. Falling not more than 300 yards from where Bob, Tom and I killed our bulls the previous year, it was pure ecstasy to be reliving such a dream.

Following a celebratory photo session, we quartered the bull and hung the meat along with the 307-inch, 6x6 rack, high in the trees, out of grizzly bear reach. We'd return the following day with horses to pack out the meat, but with six hours left in the day, it was time for me to hunt.

By mid-afternoon Bob and I had talked to more than a dozen bulls. More than half of these were coming to the calls, only to be tipped-off to our presence by unrelenting, swirling winds. Hoping to escape the wind, we dropped into a deep draw.

Losing elevation wasn't an easy decision to make. One thing I've learned about early season elk hunting is that if you can find bulls in good numbers, chances are they will be hanging out at the same elevation throughout entire drainages. Our goal was to escape the squirly winds without losing too much elevation so we could still target these bulls just above the 9,500-foot mark.

Bob Wells' opening morning bull was just shy of 310 inches.

Quickly we gave up about 500-feet, dropping near the very bottom of the timberline. We weren't out of the wind, yet, but a bugling bull above us got our attention. Unable to resist the temptation we moved closer to the bull and started calling. We knew it could be a mistake, but had to at least try.

Not only did the bull respond, but two other bulls fired back. The wind was whipping around harder with every passing moment and we knew what the outcome would be. Rather than force things, we dropped lower. There, we sat for two hours praying the wind would let up. It never did.

Cinching up our packs, we headed out of the timber. It was one of the most depressing moments of my hunting career. Here we were, miles into the backcountry, surrounded by big bulls, yet the wind kept giving us fits. It simply wasn't worth the risk of educating more bulls as we'd already done several times that day.

Hunting at such high elevation, even in early September, there was no predicting what the weather would do. I hated leaving that mountain.

We'd not gone 300 yards when a bull let out a bugle that cut through the 25 mile-per-hour winds. We were on the very edge of the timber, the surrounding trees whipping with fury in the blustery winds.

The forest was noisy, masking our sound as we quickly moved to within 75 yards of where we thought the bull was. Bob delivered a single cow call. Before the call was lost in the wind, the bull hammered right back with a double bugle and a long, raspy chuckle. No doubt he was a mature animal. We just needed the wind to stay in our faces.

Over the next five minutes the bull would answer our calls two more times, then he went silent. Certain he was approaching, my greatest fear was that he'd try circling around our backside, trying to catch our wind, or that the winds would shift and give us away.

After 10 minutes and no responses, movement from where the bull had been calling caught my eye. At first it was hard to decipher amid all the flailing limbs. Then, rays of sunlight slashing through the dark timber were broken by a massive set of antlers working our way. The rangefinder gave a firm reading of 40 yards to the trail on which the bull was moving.

Taking in a deep breath, the sounds of howling winds and crashing branches were blocked from my mind as I effortlessly brought the BowTech Patriot to full-draw. When the bull hit my yardage mark, my

*This 335" bull ended one of the most emotional,
and challenging, elk hunts of my life.*

40-yard pin quickly found his chest. Instantly the Pro 400 arrow was on it's way. The 100 grain broadhead cut through both lungs, dropping the bull on its third lunge, nine yards from where he was hit.

It was the fastest I'd ever seen a bull die. Later inspection found the arrow protruding from the back right hip of the bull. To me, this was an amazing testimony as to how tough Gold Tip arrows are. When I shot the bull, he was perfectly broadside, moving from right to left. The arrow hit the mark, right behind the shoulder, but when I saw the bull collapse so quickly, it boggled me.

Come to find out, the arrow did pierce both lungs. But for some reason, when the arrow met a rib at some point, it took a 90° turn, punched through the diaphragm, drove through the liver, then nearly exited above the opposite hip joint on the back side. That explained why the bull dropped so fast. How that arrow turned at such a severe angle without breaking, I'll never know.

The labor-intensive butchering and arduous four mile hike back to camp was less taxing than anticipated; no doubt our success and the fact we'd caught all the action on film for the American Archer TV

Some day I hope to return to this elk
hunting paradise in Wyoming's Absaroka Range.

show, played a large part in that. Throughout the night and in to the next morning, driving rains made for a miserable time. When the storm broke, we lead four horses into the hole and got all our meat safely back to camp. It was an all day task that was far from easy.

That night, seven inches of snow fell. With Tom's bow out of commission, we agreed it was best to get off the mountain and get the meat taken care of.

Lashing that 335-inch rack on to the last horse, I couldn't have been more pleased. It was a physically demanding and mentally draining hunt; one filled with numerous emotional highs and lows. Tom's bow getting destroyed was a bad deal, but not nearly as tragic as it could have been.

Good friends, demanding country and large bulls...that's what this wilderness elk hunt was all about. Every time I glance at that bull's head on my office wall, I'm reminded of just how special elk hunting truly is throughout the American West.

Chapter 19:

Turkey Time

Classified as big game in some states, small game in others, there's no question turkey hunting continues to rapidly grow in popularity. When it comes to bowhunting these keen-eyed birds, it's not easy, which is why they are so addicting.

Well before first light I had the pop-up blind in place. In front of me were two decoys–a strutting tom and a submissive hen. I was situated on a small, open, grassy knoll surround by young oak trees. On the big hillside above were mature Douglas fir trees, barely over 100 yards from where I sat.

To the east of me an old stand of white oaks covered the ridge, and to the south, a mix of hardwood and deciduous trees lined a beautiful river. The night before I'd let out some owl hoots and roosted birds in each of the stands of trees. The best part, now that I was settled in my blind with morning fast approaching, the birds were still on their roost, talking like crazy.

Hen yelps, tom yelps and gobbles filled the valley as the starry sky gave way to orange hues on the horizon. White, purple and yellow wildflowers came to life in the meadow, and the sounds of happy robins and other songbirds reminded me of why I love spring turkey hunting so much.

As minutes passed and shooting light drew near, I started announcing my presence with some alluring hen yelps. Each sound I made drew aggressive gobbles from all directions. During my roosting session the night before, I counted three flocks of birds. On this morning, once I fired-up things with some calling, I could pinpoint eight distinct flocks, all on the roost.

It was one of those times when you knew the hunt was going to come together as planned, and come together it did. Once the birds started hitting the ground it was an all-out rush for some of them to reach the decoys.

First came a flock of four toms from the east. Once they caught sight of the decoys, they stopped, puffed up their chests and pirouetted around one another. At the same time, a group of six toms approached from the north. When they saw the other toms in full-strut, they too, broke into a courtship dance and slowly walked my way.

In the distance, down by the river, a large flock of toms gobbled with every stride they made, coming right for me. Never had I heard so many gobbles simultaneously light-up a valley. At this point, none of the toms were within bow range, but I knew it was just a matter of time.

Taking in the stunning display, I really didn't want it to end. Watching the birds to my left out one window of the blind, and the toms in front out another window, I was shocked when a trio of longbeards came strutting by within 10 yards of the blind, headed for the decoys.

The three birds never did gobble, and the first signs that gave them away were their spitting and drumming. Seconds after hearing those unique sounds, the birds popped into view.

There are few sites that rival that of a mature tom strutting his way into the decoys.

Letting them pass, all three toms were puffed-up, beards dragging the ground. They wasted no time challenging the decoys, and strutted right up to them. One of the toms brushed up against the strutting tom decoy, while the others worked around in front of the hen decoy.

With these aggressive moves being made, all the toms within sight began filtering toward the decoys. In all, 13 mature toms and six jakes, all of which were nearly within bow range, moved my direction and I could hear more gobbling in the distance.

When one of the big toms fanned his tail and turned his back to me, I anchored my BowTech General. Putting my 20 yard pin at the very base of the tom's tail, where all the tail feathers converged, I touched my release.

Silently my Gold Tip arrow slid from the bow, then hit the bird with a resounding "whack!" The last thing I saw was my white fletching being consumed by fluffy tail feathers. The shot came at 11 yards, and set at 70 pounds, the two-blade expandable was driven completely through the big bird.

The number of toms that approached
the decoys on this morning made for a memorable turkey hunt.

Upon impact my bird jumped, stacked his feathers, then looked around as if to say, "What just happened?" Then he took a few steps and his groggy body collapsed. The two toms that were with him took off, but just as quickly, four approaching toms attacked him.

Unfortunately, I was only allowed a bird a day on this spring hunt, otherwise I could have filled all three tags in my pocket right then and there. Instead, I sat, watching the displays of the other birds over my expired tom.

In acts of dominance, the four toms beat and tormented the corpse, ripping feathers from him, stomping on him, spurring him and even pecking at his head. Not wanting them to damage the meat, I soon put a stop to it.

In terms of turkey action, and observing turkey behavior, that was one of the most memorable turkey hunts of my life. I've been fortunate to take several turkeys with a my bow over the years, and never tire of the challenge these nervous birds offer.

Because their feathers can be pulled tight to their bodies, creating an almost armor-like shield, and due to the fact a turkey's bones are hollow and so rigid, I choose to shoot my big game setup when hunting turkeys. I use the same bow, pull the same poundage and rely on the same arrows as I do for most big game, including elk. It's certainly not necessary to shoot the same setup used for big game, just a personal preference of mine. Many people prefer dropping their poundage for turkeys, whereby allowing them to hold more steadily and more easily reach full-draw when hunkered in a blind. The only difference, I'll use an expandable broadhead on turkeys.

Personally, I'm not a big fan of expandables on big game, but on turkeys, they are perfect. Their cut-on-impact heads and large cutting area make expandables the ideal head of choice for turkeys.

In addition, turkeys have one of the smallest kill-zones of any game animal, and if you don't hit the spot, chances of losing that bird are high. These are tough critters and just because they're a bird doesn't mean you can get lazy with shot placement. Shoot an arrow with field point accuracy, hit the money-spot and let the expandable do the work; that's your goal when bowhunting for turkeys.

A great joy of hunting turkeys, be it spring or fall, is what they teach you. I can't think of any other animal that will hone the skills of big game hunters like a turkey can. Their eyesight is second to none, their nervous behavior constantly keeps the hunter focused and the fact you can have multiple encounters during a single day's hunt, means the amount of learning that can take place is immense.

One spring I tagged all three of my Oregon toms with a bow. One of the birds came from a treestand, one from the ground via spot-and-stalk and the other from a ground blind. If I had one choice of cover from which to bowhunt turkeys, it would be a ground blind. Ground blinds mask your movement like nothing else can, allowing you to reach full-draw without being seen. I also like using decoys to stop the birds in a good shooting position.

On a hunt for Merriam's turkey in Montana, I spent two hours calling from a ground blind. Though toms gobbled to nearly all my sounds, they never came in. After nearly three hours the birds shut-down so I folded up the blind and left. I'd gone about 100 yards then glanced back at the hillside near where my blind had been set. That's when I saw a lone tom, skirting the edge of the ridge.

Quickly I dropped into a creek bottom and beat feet back to where I'd had the blind set. Wasting no time, I again erected the blind and started calling. By now, mid-day winds were howling in excess of 30 miles per hour. I heard the tom gobble once, but he sounded a long way off. When his patriotic-colored head broke the horizon line 20 yards in front of me, I about choked on my diaphragm call.

He continued moving right at me, and though I was at full-draw, couldn't get a shot. Had I set a decoy in front of me, I'm confident the tom would have stopped and strutted his stuff. He never did break into a strut, and never quit moving. Fearing he'd move off, I made sure my kisser button was in the corner of my lip, and that I could clearly see the tom through my peep, then I let out a soft yelp on the diaphragm call.

Pulling his feathers tight and standing tall, the bird was nervous, curious as to why he could hear hen yelps less than 10 yards away, but couldn't see her. At that instant I released the arrow and drove it through the shoulder of the tom. He went seven yards and tipped over. I learned two lessons that day: be patient when working a place you know birds are at, and be sure to have a diaphragm call in your mouth to stop birds when in optimal shooting position.

Two of my most memorable turkey hunts came when I didn't have my bow with me. One was a fall hunt, where my wife, Tiffany, was carrying her BowTech Mighty Mite. We'd been scouting a flock of birds making their usual rounds gathering food. Turkeys are much easier to

High winds made for tough hunting, but persistence paid off for me on this Montana Merriam's turkey.

pattern in the fall than in spring, and we felt good about the prospects of getting Tiffany a shot.

Tiffany is a busy lady. A full-time mom of our two boys—three, counting me—and a cookbook author, she runs our family business, books my speaking engagements and travel for the TV show, edits all of my articles and books, runs our household, cooks all our family meals and still manages to break free for a hunt now and then. Her time is very valuable, so I'm happy when a hunting plan comes together.

Based on our scouting, the flock of turkeys were working down a powerline right-of-way about 9:00 every morning. So, by 8:30 a.m. we were huddled together in a ground blind, waiting for the birds to walk down the trail, just as they'd been doing for the past two weeks.

Sure enough, right on schedule–actually, a few minutes early–here came the flock of more than 20 birds, pecking their way down the treeline. It was a mix of jakes and hens, both of which are legal in the fall. Tiffany was in the middle of writing a bird cookbook and didn't care about tagging a mature tom, she just wanted something for the pot as turkey meat is one of our family favorites.

As the flock approached, Tiffany nocked an arrow and got comfortable. The first few turkeys came in to range, and Tiff' was ready to launch an arrow, but they wouldn't stop. Then they began picking clover and grass, 25 yards in front of us. A few jakes veered from the flock, feeding closer to our blind. At 20 yards, Tiffany picked a spot on an unknowing jake and let loose. The arrow passed through the bird and feathers filled the air.

The flock ran off into the timber, and Tiff's bird tried keeping up, but it never made it to the trees. We had fresh turkey for dinner that night. Sometimes turkey hunts happen just as planned.

My most memorable turkey hunt of all time was with my then six year old son, Braxton. We were back east working on some projects for BowTech's TV show I used to host. Braxton had his bow on the trip, and we made time to chase fall turkeys.

My wife, Tiffany, and her first turkey taken with a bow.

Braxton, age six, with his first turkey arrowed from a ground blind. We captured this hunt on film for BowTech's Western Adventures, a show I used to host on the Men's Channel.

Again, we'd patterned the birds and set up a ground blind in their path of travel. On day one the birds skirted by, out of range. On day two, a small flock of hens crossed the fence right at the corner where we had our blind. One hen walked only a few inches from the blind. The expression on Braxton's face was priceless, and he remained statue-still and absolutely quiet.

More birds walked by, then, finally one stopped at 11 yards. Braxton had a shot at her back and drove the arrow home. The bird took off running under a fence, through a dry creek bottom and into some brush 40 yards away. Braxton was concerned, but after finding his arrow and learning a bit on how to track hit game, he found his bird, dead under an old snag. The hen sported a six-inch beard and marked the beginning of Braxton's love of turkey hunting.

What being in the spring turkey woods is all about!

There have been other memorable turkey hunts over the years, including the the one I spot-and-stalked as it strutted around a band of hens. I couldn't get any closer as the birds moved into an open meadow, so let the arrow fly. I was shooting my BowTech Tribute, set at nearly 80 pounds. I was shooting the bow well, and it was launching my arrows with impressive speed and accuracy.

When ranging the bird at 64 yards, I felt good about taking the shot. With the TV camera's rolling, the bird unaware of our presence, I let loose. Bingo, the arrow hit the mark. The bird whirled, tumbled, then took to the air. It was only airborne a short distance, then it fell from the sky.

Going after turkeys, bow in-hand, is one of hunting's greatest joys. The settings, the physical ease of the hunt and the willingness of the birds to respond to calls in breathtaking fashion is something a turkey hunter never tires of. Be it spring or fall, there is much to be learned from spending time in the turkey woods. Once you hunt them, you'll gain a more clear understanding of why the wild turkey nearly became our national bird.

Chapter 20:

B.C. Black Bears

*Having hunted multiple places in Canada
for black bears, there's one that stands out in my mind, a place I
can't wait to get back to.*

Walking the edge of a logging road, a distinct black color caught our eye. It was much darker than the burned stumps that had been fooling us, and when it finally moved, left no question as to what it was.

"The wind is perfect, I think you can go right up the ditchline and get within range of that bear," whispered Rob Cork, owner of Tweedsmuir Park Outfitters in British Columbia. Rob stayed back, watching through his binoculars while I edged forward.

I first ranged the bear at 70 yards and knew then I'd be able to get much closer. The soft grass and thick patches of lush clover made for quiet walking and so far the wind held steady.

At 40 yards a bright red bush caught my attention behind the bear. It glowed in the golden hour of twilight, and I passed it off as a bush that had been scorched by slash burning. Focusing my attention back on the big black bear, the red bush got up and moved. It was the brightest colored cinnamon bear I'd ever seen, and had been obscured by brush and tall grass up to this point of the stalk.

Had it not been a sow, I'd have arrowed that thing on the spot. As it were, the sow walked, plucked some fresh sprigs of grass and vanished into the forest. It was the last day of May and the bear rut was kicking in. Over the past two days we'd seen an increase in boar movement and knowing this, I feared my black boar would follow his red-haired girlfriend into the trees.

A cinnamon phase black bear enjoys a mouth full of fresh dandelions along the edge of a logging road.

Positioning for a shot, the last range I took read 35 yards. The boar seemed to pay no attention to the sow as he was sprawled out on his belly, relishing in the bountiful grass.

Then he stood and turned straight away. He was in no hurry and had a good 10 yards to go before reaching the timber. By now I was drawn, waiting for him to turn broadside. He was a big bear, his ebony hide no doubt squaring over seven feet. The moment he started to turn, he hit a low spot, covering his vitals. Now all I could see was his back. A few strides later and he was in the brush, never to be seen again.

Fifteen minutes later we were stalking another bear. Though this one wasn't as big, he was in a good, stalkable position, so I went for it. By the time I got to within range, I could see he wasn't as big as I'd originally thought, so I let him walk.

Shortly after, a monster bear fed in the road. He was also well over the seven foot mark and when he ducked into some willows in a ditch bordering the logging road, I made a move. Figuring the brute would come out and start feeding again, within bow range, he failed to show. I hit the predator calls for over 10 minutes and still, nothing.

Going into the brush after him, Rob soon spotted the bear grazing on grass in a logged unit, 200 yards up the hill. That old bear knew where he was going and didn't want to have anything to do with us. I would have loved taking that bear, he was giant.

As the evening hunt came to a close we reflected on the many bears we'd seen over the previous six days. We already had two Game Chasers TV shows in the can and were working on a third. The first two shows were rifle hunts, where both my wife and 10 year old son, Braxton, took their first bears. Both of their bears pushed squaring the seven foot mark and I took a monster chocolate bear that went over seven feet. In all we'd seen 35 black bears and four grizzlies.

We were hunting a new chunk of land Rob was considering purchasing for his outfitting business, and all liked what we were seeing. In Canada, outfitters own the land they hunt, but don't take that to mean these are small parcels of real estate. The block we hunted was nearly 900,000 acres, and that butted up against his already existing concession of 1 million acres. It's more land than can be hunted in a lifetime, but where we were, the bears were thick.

We were on a remote, interior island. Technically it wasn't an island, as a narrow, 200 yard strip of ground connected it to the mainland. Separated by Ootsa Lake, the only way to reach this supposedly unnamed island is by boat. Prior to our arrival, Rob had barged in a couple trucks for us to hunt from. The cabins were already in place, thanks to the previous outfitter Rob was considering buying from.

The level of activity on the island had been low for years. The previous outfitter hadn't hunted the land for five years and commercial logging stopped a year prior to that. This meant the bears in this vast tract of land hadn't seen humans for five years. An outfitter had been hunting the other half of the island but with very few hunters each year and on more land than he could cover in several seasons. In other words, the pressure is about as low as it gets.

What made this place so special to hunt was the intricate web of gravel logging roads that weaved about the island. Here, the logging roads are the lifeline for bears in the spring.

This far north–about a five hour drive northwest of Prince George– bears spend nearly six months in their den. When they emerge, their fat supplies have greatly dwindled and immediately the bears gravitate to where the most nutritious foods are found, along logging roads.

As winter snow melts and spring rains fall, runoff along the logging roads delivers high amounts of moisture, whereby allowing grass and other food sources to flourish. Combine this with the extended amount of springtime sunlight reaching the open spaces along the logging roads, and plant life thrives even more. Rain plus sun equals photosynthesis, and the plant life growing along the logging roads greatly surpasses that found in logged units and meadows this time of year.

Bears gravitate to the logging roads at lower elevations where it's warmer and where grasses first sprout. Clover and dandelions also grow here and are valued spring food sources of bears. Find a place offering grass, clover and dandelions, and you're just about assured of finding bears as long as there is some thick cover nearby where they can seek safety.

One thing that did surprise me was how edgy the bears were. "There are so many grizzlies here, they really put the black bears on alert," shared Cork. "The biggest of the big black bears might not be afraid of

Grass, dandelions and clover flourish along logging roads where runoff is high.

the grizzlies, and they can be more approachable than the smaller black bears." Rob was right.

By 5:00 the next morning we were driving logging roads and looking for bears. The first bear we saw was a dandy black. To this point four of the more than 30 bears we'd seen were cinnamon or chocolate color phase. Rob stopped the truck and Travis Ralls, my camera man, and I quietly slipped out and began our stalk.

Working our way up the opposite ditchline, we knew we'd be close when we popped on to the road. In many places the logging roads had been built-up with gravel, greatly elevating them above the bordering ditches. This not only created great places for the runoff to collect, allowing plant life to prosper, but it also made for the perfect stalking situation. Being able to stay low and remain unseen until the moment of the shot definitely gives the bowhunter a needed advantage.

When Travis and I poked our heads above the road, the bear was gone. Slowly we moved forward, then caught sight of his back. He'd dropped down into the opposite ditch and was drinking from a small pool of water. Figuring he'd step back on to the grassy road when done, we held steady, ready for the shot. The moment the bear started moving I drew, heart thumping hard in my chest. The bear was only 11 yards from me and if he continued moving forward, would be eight steps from my broadhead before I let it fly.

But the bear turned and paralleled the ditch. We moved forward, trying to head him off but he slipped behind a curtain of young pine trees. At 10 yards all we could catch were glimpses of the bear, one we figured would have squared right at or just over seven feet. He was a massive bear but unfortunately we never got a shot at him.

Shortly after that encounter we watched a gorgeous chocolate bear moving across a logged unit. There was an old skid road running through the unit and it was covered in grass and clover. Given all the brush laying on the ground and the open country between the bear and us, there was no prayer of getting to within range of him.

Rounding a few corners in the road we stumbled upon the biggest bear of the trip. "That bear will go at least 7'10", Rob blurted out. "He's one of the biggest bears I've seen in my entire life!"

To this point, between the three bears my family had in camp and those from other hunters, Rob had been judging these bears with stunning accuracy. The bears this far north are much skinnier and longer legged than what I'm used to hunting in Oregon, Washington and Idaho this time to year, and I was under-judging them by nearly a foot at times. It's not fair to gauge them in pounds in the spring, as they burn about 30% of their total body weight during winter. Squared measurements are the most accurate way to field judge these bears and Rob had it down, calling every single bear we'd killed to this point within an inch.

When Rob perked up over the sight of that big bear, Travis and I wasted no time getting to work. The bear saw us, though, and scampered into some trees. Hoping he'd come back out to feed, we quickly covered ground. Sure enough, the bear emerged from the timber. He was only 100 yards away but the road had no ditch, meaning we were 100% exposed with no way of getting closer.

When the bear finally fed out of sight we moved forward again. This time he busted us for good, and despite spending half the day trying to find him, we never did see that brute again.

By working the sunken ditchlines of logging roads, stalking bears is a high percentage proposition in this part of British Columbia.

It wasn't long and our spirits were lifted as we stumbled upon another bear. This one barely pushed the six foot mark but I didn't care as he seemed less nervous than some of the other's we'd encountered. He cruised the road at a good clip, more intent on locating a fertile sow than amassing greens. Given his aggressive stature, we tried calling.

The minute my lips hit the open reeded Last Call, the bear stopped, did a 180 and came our way. Travis and I tucked into some brush along the edge of the road while Rob backed off 30 yards in an attempt to call and pull the bear past us.

As the bear continued coming to my squealing sounds, he crossed the road and walked along the same ditch we were hiding in. Should he continue along that path he'd be within five yards of me by the time I'd be able to shoot.

Once the bear hit the 30 yard mark I felt certain I'd soon be placing my tag on him. Then, suddenly, he stopped, sniffed the air and grew nervous. Instantly he stood on his hind legs, wet, black nose pumping hard in the slight breeze. I didn't have a shot through the brush, but it didn't matter, for as quickly as it all began, it ended.

The bear ducked into the brush behind us. We could hear him breaking branches as he skirted around our calling site, trying to confirm our presence with the wind. Then all went quiet. Figuring he'd walked off, we gathered our gear and headed back to the truck. That's the instant the bear hopped back on to the logging road, 25 yards behind us. By the time we got the camera rolling, it was too late, the bear was gone for good this time.

Driving back to the cabin for lunch, a small bear crossed the road in front of us. A few miles down the road another bear did the same thing, this one bigger than the last. "That's not a bad bear," I pointed out. "He'll go a bit over six feet," Rob affirmed.

Urging Rob to stop the truck I let it be known I'd be happy with that bear. We'd seen many great bears during our hunt, and I've been fortunate to take some whoppers over the years, so was content with the bear we'd just seen. Besides, work back home beckoned me and I was getting anxious to wrap-up this hunt.

Again, Travis and I hopped out of the truck and slipped into the ditch. We quickly covered 125 yards and the moment we saw the bear, he rambled off. He wasn't on an all-out sprint, just slightly nervous. He moved into a logged unit and we followed. That's when I put the Last Call between my teeth and cut loose.

My longtime camera man, Travis Ralls, and I with our spring B.C. bear.
Travis and I have shared many great memories around the world while filming
for our Game Chasers T.V. show.

BOWHUNTING THE WEST & BEYOND

The high-pitched sounds caught his attention and he stopped immediately. He was just over 100 yards away and I figured we didn't have a prayer of closing the deal. But we had to at least try.

With Travis tight to my backside, continuously rolling tape, I frantically called with every step we took. There was no masking our steps in the dry, brush-covered ground. We simply accepted the noise of our walking and I blew on the call as aggressively as I could.

To our amazement the bear held his ground. He didn't come any closer, and I didn't expect him to. At this point all I was hoping for was that he'd stay put, letting me slip within bow range.

We ducked into a little depression and lost sight of the bear for several seconds. When we popped up, he was still in the same place. By now the vegetation was sparse and I knew we couldn't get any closer.

Picking a hole between the two little pine trees behind which the bear stood, I got three consistent readings of 72 yards. I'd been shooting my new BowTech Destroyer well, and given the fact I was on level ground with no wind, I drew.

With my bow set at over 70 pounds and pushing a Gold Tip Pro 400 arrow at 325 feet per second, I was relieved to see the white vanes smack the black hide behind the bear's left shoulder. The Slick Trick broadhead did the job and after a quick sprint into the nearby timber, we soon found the bear piled-up beneath some blowdowns. The family would be heading home with four bears, plenty of meat for the freezers and some of the best pelts I've ever run my fingers through.

While I've not yet hunted British Columbia's Vancouver Island, I can't imagine many places surpassing what this slice of paradise has to offer. On this remote island of the interior could well be not only British Columbia's best kept bear secret, but one of the premier up-and-coming spots for avid bear hunters to explore. Based on what I saw, I can't wait to get back and hunt these bears, for there are some true giants lurking in those forests.

Chapter 21:

Hawaiian Boar & Billies

Hawaii. It's almost as far West as you can go and still be in the United States, and far enough south you're in paradise. More than sun and sandy beaches, Hawaii is an overlooked hunting destination I can never get enough of.

After a lengthy walk through tall, lush grass and ankle-grabbing vines, we finally broke into the open. Climbing up a gentle knoll of exposed, black lava rock, my camera man, Dave Arabia, and I soon crested the hill.

Before us was one of the most striking settings I'd ever laid eyes on; the kind that truly takes your breath away. No words were spoken, nor necessary, largely because none could describe the feeling, the beauty, the serenity of that moment.

There we stood, gazing across the shimmering silver surface of the Pacific Ocean. Water stretched as far as the eye could see. Where the radiant sun plunged toward the western horizon, a band of fiery-orange hues transformed the water's surface. Around us, rich, green, chest-high grass glowed, making our surroundings unusually bright. It was a setting we just stared at in awe.

As the warm, salty, ocean breeze drifted up from the cliffs below, the distinct smell of goats filled my nostrils. Taking a few steps forward, my stomach turned at the sight of the near vertical, 500-foot drop. Below, the crashing waves foamed against the ebony lava, deep, aqua-blue pools surrounding them. It only added to the beauty of the moment.

Suddenly, the cry of goats caught my ears. The sights and smells left no question goats were near, we just had to find them.

With it's rugged, razor-like lava cliffs, Hawaii is unlike any place I've hunted.

Dave and I were filming the pilot episode of Adventures Abroad, a show I hosted during its first season on the Outdoor Channel. We were hunting on the Big Island of Hawaii, along the Kona Coast. More specifically, we were hunting at the base of Mauna Loa volcano, where this active mountain dumped into the crystal-clear waters of the Pacific.

Though we were at sea level, we were far from the base of the volcano. From its summit, some 13,500-feet, to where it stems from the ocean floor, Mauna Loa is the largest shield volcano in the world, encompassing approximately 18,000 cubic miles. Under water, the mountain creates one of the richest ocean fisheries on the planet; above water, its varied habitat makes for some of the best goat, sheep and hog hunting in the nation.

Camera rolling, Dave and I inched closer to the cliff's edge, intent on finding the goats we could smell and hear below us. Finally, a glimpse of black caught my eye...then another. I was surprised at how coal black the bodies of the goats were, blending in to the lava rock so well it made seeing them difficult, until they moved.

Closer to the edge I nudged, until I could see well over 100 head of goats picking their way through trails etched into the lava. I kept counting goats that strung out along the flow beneath us. Some were simply standing in the rocks, seemingly taking in the captivating sunset as I'm sure they do every evening, while others fed along the grassy edges, more intent on filling their bellies. I quit counting at 300 head, and there were more continually pouring out of the brush and rocky cliffs below.

The whole setting was so surreal, I was jolted back to reality when Dave snuck up close to me and whispered, "Are there any shooters in there?" Too wrapped-up in the moment, I'd all but forgotten about shooting.

As I glassed the largest band of goats, just over 100 yards below us, I could hear more in the brush. I could see the grass moving, but it was so tall, it enveloped the goats, making it impossible to see them.

Then, boldly, a band of black goats came striding onto an exposed lava outcropping, not 60 yards below. Nocking an arrow, I anchored, then touched my release. All I can remember seeing was my white fletching sailing toward the black rocks, illuminated by the setting sun.

The shot felt good and the goats had no idea we were there. But when my Gold Tip, graphite arrow exploded on the lava, goats scurried in every direction. The shot was almost straight downhill, and my lack of compensation for the steep angle sent the arrow just over the back of a large-horned billy. There was no second chance, not on this herd.

Eighteenth century Spanish explorers first brought goats to the Hawaiian Islands. In those days goats were planted all over islands throughout the South Pacific, creating a continual food source explorers could rely on during their subsequent return trips.

Today, Spanish goats are found throughout much of Hawaii, for they thrive in this food-rich, comfortable climate. Other than a few wild dogs and some hogs, these goats have no natural predators so their propensity to reproduce with minimal loss is impressive.

The next day we were back at it, trying to secure my first Spanish goat in Hawaii. It was mid-morning by the time we reached the hunting grounds and the day was already heating up. Fresh beds and rubs were permeated with the stench of rutting billy goats, leaving no question we were in the right place.

Due to the already intense heat, the goat herds had moved from their open, early morning feeding grounds into the brushy thickets

*Goats are plentiful on various Hawaiian Islands, making
for nonstop hunting action.*

where shade offered relief. Following our noses along the well-worn goat
trails carved deep into the exposed lava from hundreds of years of travel,
the going was easy.

Then, in the distance we heard the sounds of goats. In this thick,
coastal habitat, goats are very vocal. The nannies and kids are almost
in continual communication in an effort to maintain contact with one
another. Even for goats it's easy getting separated in this tangled, brushy
land.

One herd in particular sounded off a couple hundred yards above
us. Moving their direction, we picked our way along the trail, through
low-growing brush. As we broke into a small opening, movement off to
the left caught my eye.

Dropping to one knee, I nocked an arrow as the camera was readied.
Another flicker of an ear left no question a herd of goats was moving
our direction. This wasn't the same herd we were stalking on, rather
another small group traveling the same trail we were, but in the opposite
direction.

First a small nanny popped into view, then I could see the horns of a
small billy close behind. Ranging the nanny, I got a reading of 19 yards.
A few animals back, I could see the horns of a bigger billy, but given the

fact they were moving my way, fast, I figured they'd bust me by the time I could get a shot on the large billy.

Instead, I decided to take the first billy, the one behind the lead nanny. As the nanny cleared, I reached full-draw. In preparation for an upcoming trip to Africa, I had my BowTech Allegiance set at 82 pounds. Chronographing at 333 feet-per-second, it was an overkill for these goats but what I needed for some of the dangerous game we'd soon be hunting on the Dark Continent.

Lots of animals and multiple stalking opportunities each day make hunting Hawaii's goats a valuable experience for the bowhunter.

Looking at my 20 yard pin, it was rock-solid, and before I knew it my bow fired, almost with surprise. The fletch was swallowed by the billy's jet-black pelage and he wasted no time sprinting downhill.

Following the blood trail was simple and short. The billy only made it 15 yards before plowing into a tree. Though he was far from the biggest billy on the block, I'd finally drawn blood.

After quartering the goat–the locals love their goat meat–and a short snack, a mid-day monsoon hit. Heavy rain pelted us for nearly an hour, just as it had been doing each of the past few days at the very same time. We were there during the 4th of July, a festive time for sure, but one where heavy rains routinely make their presence known in the hottest part of the day.

As the rain began to let up, we moved on. I hadn't gone 50 yards when a baby goat came running up to me. Nestling into my legs the kid obviously mistook me for it's mother. Kneeling down, I reached out my hand, and the kid burrowed into it. It seemed quite content, and failed to acknowledge the cries of its real mother in the distance.

Finally, the nanny came looking for her lost kid. I picked up the pace, hoping to out-walk the kid, but it didn't work. It kept up with me, stride for stride. When the nanny came into view and saw her baby following me, she didn't like it one bit. Full-steam she sprinted down the lava face, head down, bearing right at me.

I juked to one side. She didn't buy it. But, she did stop, finally. A mere three yards from me she stood, hackles high, nostrils flared, glaring at her kid. Then the little guy caught wind of her and hopped to her side. I walked away, the kid stayed with his mom.

Farther down the trail, I came face-to-face with another nanny. This one had her head down, pushing into the driving rain which had intensified. She was on the same trail I was, so I just stopped and let her come. Behind her was a nice billy but he only had one horn.

They were headed to the caves to escape the torrential rains. Less than two feet from me she finally stopped, then made an aggressive posture as she recognized I shouldn't have been there. It wouldn't have bothered me too much, but I was actually in a very bad spot. I had stopped on the edge of a vertical cliff; one step back would have sent me more than 300-feet down the jagged lava face and into the crashing ocean waves. And with all the rain, the rocks were slippery.

Knowing goats can be aggressive, I anticipated a head-on confrontation. But just as the nanny postured, she whirled and ran off. It was a shot of adrenaline I never thought I'd receive, not on a goat hunt.

The goats, several hundred of them, were now pouring off the hillside, headed for the safety of the many caves which were carved into the ocean cliffs. Most caves are inaccessible to humans, but the goats make their cliff-hopping antics seem effortless, whereby reaching them with ease. It was one of the most amazing spectacles of animals seeking shelter that I'd ever witnessed.

The goats hate rain, and staying dry was their only concern. Taking a seat, I didn't mind the rain, in fact, it felt refreshing in the sweltering heat. I was concerned about the camera, however. We were shooting with a state-of-the-art camera, a Sony F900, which, combined with a specialty set of lenses and a spendy tripod, were worth about $240,000 at the time. But the camera man assured me it was sealed tight and the rain shouldn't be a problem.

So, I picked a trail and waited for the storm to pass. Once the rains quit I reasoned that the goats would emerge from the caves and climb back up to higher ground. No sooner had the rains subsided when the first goats crawled out from the caves. They wasted no time heading up the hill, either.

What amazed me most was the number of caves hidden within the ocean cliffs. From one point, we could look into the bay below and see the memorial where Captain Cook had been slain. The land we hunted was rich in history, and culture, making it even more special.

From every ocean cliff, herds of goats worked their way up the jagged lava flows. I was surprised at how fast they moved, knowing I'd have to do the same if I wanted to get another billy.

Spotting a stalkable herd, we took off. The group got past us, but they moved slow in the steep draw they found themselves in. Taking the opportunity, I climbed as quickly as I could, the sharp, glass-like lava slicing my boots like no rocks ever had. Heart pounding, legs burning, I ranged the last billy in the herd at 46 yards. Though he was standing still, the front of the herd was moving, so I knew I didn't have much time to let an arrow fly.

As the Allegiance sent another Gold Tip on its way, it promptly disappeared behind the last rib. With the billy quartering away, facing uphill, the shot felt good. The goat went a few steps and bedded down, then I drove home an insurance shot. Pound for pound these goats are as tough as any ungulate I know of and I didn't want to risk losing this one.

On the goat's final death kick, he sent himself over a cliff, sliding down a lava chute. He finally came to rest more than 200 feet below. There was no way we could follow as these lava cliffs are among the most unstable of all the worlds mountains to traverse. In fact, prior to my arrival, a friend had lost his son on such a cliff.

Far from the biggest Spanish goat I saw, I was pleased to recover this one after a lengthy fall down a steep lava flow.

The young man–a seasoned hunter in the area–had shot a goat and went across the lava flow to recover it. But before he could finish the job, the lava gave way, sending him several hundred feet down the cliff. It was a brutal ending and a reminder to all hunters how unforgiving the land can be that we hunt...even in Hawaii.

Hiking off the mountain, we finally found our goat piled-up in a pocket of giant boulders, not far from the rushing shoreline. Fortunately, his horns were intact and his body not too battered. We had more meat to give the locals, which pleased everyone.

The next day we headed up the volcano, well above the 5,000-foot level. This terrain was far different than where we'd spent the previous two days. Though lava was still present, it was grown over by thick, jungle-like rainforest. Along with the change in topography came a change in prey, as this time our target species was the prized Polynesian boar.

I'd hoped to find a boar by way of spot-and-stalk, but the habitat was simply too dense. Getting a pack of hounds increased our chances of success, and that afternoon we headed back up the hill, dogs in tow.

It didn't take long and the dogs had a strike. As a kid I relished every hound hunt I was fortunate to be a part of, as the rush is fast-paced and the close encounters like no other. Soon the hounds barked "bayed."

Closing in, it was difficult to see the hog, though he was less than 10 yards from me. Thick, wet ferns covered him and I could only catch fleeting glimpses of the hog's back and snout. I anchored two times, but simply couldn't get a shot. Then he busted loose.

The dogs wasted no time trailing the boar and after a few hundred yards had him bayed-up, again. This time the hog was on a hillside, beneath a bush that draped over his back. The dogs were working the boar from below and every time he lunged out from beneath the bush, he was in the wide-open.

My greatest concern was arrowing the boar, then having him turn on the dogs with a broadhead sticking out the other side. Given the steepness of the hillside the hog was on, I knew the arrow wouldn't pass through him, rather be stopped by dirt on the other side.

I hollered over the incessant bark of the hounds to let the local houndsmen know I didn't feel comfortable with the shot. They instructed me to take it anyway, that the dogs would get out of the way.

Just as I reached full-draw, the boar charged. In one motion I let down and ducked behind a tree. Dave got nailed in the leg, the boar

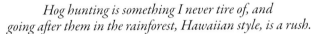

*Hog hunting is something I never tire of, and
going after them in the rainforest, Hawaiian style, is a rush.*

tearing his pant leg with it's razor sharp tusk. Fortunately the cut didn't hit Dave's leg. Just as quickly the dogs were on the boar and he retreated back beneath the bush.

Heart pounding, I quickly anchored the release under my chin. Dave gave me the thumbs-up. The instant the boar poked out from under the brush, I let the arrow fly. At only four yards the arrow didn't have far to travel before hitting its mark and burying into the opposite hillside.

Fortunately, when the arrow passed through, the broadhead broke off in some exposed roots in the dirt. Though the shaft was still in the pig, at least the

Feasting on fresh coconuts was a great way to end the hunt.

broadhead wasn't any danger to the aggressive dogs.

After a quick run around the bush, the hog was back where I'd first shot him, still snapping and snarling at the dogs. I let him have another arrow and this one helped expedite his death.

Tipping the scales to over 200 pounds, bottom tusks measuring just shy of three-inches, he was a very good boar for the area. As with all hound hunting, the chase was intense and demanding. Leading up steep hillsides, through tangled vines, thick fern patches and soaking-wet bogs, I wouldn't have expected anything less.

Dragging our wet, weary bodies off the volcano, packs full of meat, I was relieved when we came across a coconut tree. One of the local houndsmen wasted no time shimmying up the tree and slicing down both ripe and green coconuts.

As he articulated his machete's blade around the end of the green coconuts, I shucked the husk off a brown one. Soon we were sinking out teeth into fresh chunks of coconut and drinking succulent green coconut water. It was a fitting end to an enjoyable hunt, the likes of which can only be experienced in the great land of Hawaii.

Chapter 22:

Monster Red Stags of New Zealand

The South Pacific is a region teaming with some of the world's most sought-after big game, and the mighty red stag tops the list of most hunters. Little did I know that on this hunt I'd get to live the dream of hunting reds in the roar...twice!

A final check of the wind confirmed it was still in our favor. We'd already covered 250 yards, slowly and silently in the dew-laden grass of early morning.

"If you can make it up to that tree, you'll be close to 30 yards from the stag," whispered Gerald Fluerty, owner of Wildside Hunting Safaris. Gerald has made his living hunting red stags in New Zealand, first as a market meat hunter, now as one of the country's top outfitters. When he speaks, I always listen.

It felt like an eternity, but when I finally reached the big tree and looked down on the bedded stag, all I could think about was the immense size of his antlers. They dwarfed his red-hued body, curled up in a ball to conserve heat on this frosty morning.

A quick reading of the rangefinder confirmed just what Gerald had said; 35 yards. With an arrow nocked, I eased forward ever so slightly to clear the tall, yellow grass on the knob which I stood. Simultaneously reaching full-draw with my final step, I saw the stag's ears pivot on his head like mini satellite dishes. I knew then I'd blown it.

As that last step fell in the tall grass, a branch I'd not seen, snapped. The stag didn't know exactly where the sound came from, but it was enough to push him from his bed and into thick cover.

Dejected and frustrated with my mistake, I looked at Gerald who shot me a smile. It was one of the biggest red stags I'd ever seen, and carried more mass than seemed physically possible to manage.

"That's okay, there's plenty more stags around," encouraged Gerald. "Let's go try and find another one."

I was hunting at the base of Mount Ruapehu, an active volcano situated on the southern portion of New Zealand's North Island. Less than six months prior the volcano had erupted, something that constantly loomed in my mind during my week-long safari there.

It was March, peak of the red stag rut. Though I'd hunted red stag in Australia, and seen them on previous hunts to New Zealand, this was the first time I'd experienced the famed "roar."

Each and every night at camp the echoing sounds of rutting, roaring stags made getting a full-night's sleep a challenge. With so much commotion, setting foot into the wild, forested land of New Zealand before daylight each morning made it hard to decide which roaring stag to target. By mid-day the roars would wane, but pick up again as evening approached.

The March red stag roar is something every bowhunter should experience.

GERALD FLUERTY PHOTO

Sounding more like a lion than an elk, the red stag roar is something that, once you hear it, you'll never forget. The deep, guttural sounds resonate through the valleys and dense, lush timber. The lingering roars carry far, and spur other stags to respond in the same way. Hearing a half-dozen stags roaring at a time is not uncommon.

Though I'd blown the first stalk on a monster stag, I remained positive and we pushed on. Following a deep-sounding roar, Gerald and I were soon staring at a stag through our binoculars. He stood on the edge of a grassy clearing, very near heavy timber.

Given the direction of the wind there was no way of reaching the stag, not now. We watched. We listened. A few minutes and several roars later, the mighty stag melted into thick cover. As he disappeared, his hefty rack laid across his back, steam rolling from his gaping mouth as he roared. We continued on.

Throughout the rest of the day we had a several exciting stalks, but either they didn't pan-out or the animals weren't as big as we'd hoped. I must admit, after blowing it on the first stag–the biggest we'd seen thus far–I didn't want to settle for anything less. Every time I closed my eyes I could see his massive rack, points sticking every direction.

Hunting this land reminded me of where I grew up hunting Roosevelt elk in the dense Coast Range of Oregon. But there was a bit more open grassland surrounding the timber here, and the stags were regularly along these open edges, incessantly roaring.

The following morning we hiked toward a high hill, wanting to be in position by first light. This would allow us to quickly move in any direction on any good stag we might see or hear. But we didn't make it to the top.

"That's a big stag," whispered Gerald in response to a raspy, deep-voiced roar that reverberated from the valley below. We stopped and listened. With every breath it seemed the stag let out a roar. It was the most aggressive roar we'd heard and Gerald thought it would be worth checking out.

A heavy frost made for noisy going and we grew frustrated. By now our stag had been joined by another, and you could hear them moving further away with each roar. Making an aggressive move, Gerald and I picked up the pace. We'd covered more than a mile when we finally caught glimpse of one of the stags.

By now they'd quit roaring, and grazed along the edge of a meadow below us. We were more than 100 yards above the stags, and through the thick brush could only make out their bodies and parts of their racks.

"Let's move down the ridge and try getting in front of them," Gerald whispered. Confident we were lined-out on the direction the stags were moving, we made our way through the timber, down a well worn trail.

Gerald lead the way, I followed, and behind me, just as he'd been since the hunt began, was my ace camera man and co-producer, Dave Arabia. We were there to capture the hunt on film for the first ever episode of our new Game Chasers TV show, for the Outdoor Channel. What a start we were off to.

To this point we had incredible footage. Me blowing a stalk on that big stag, passing on some others and intimate images of stags roaring and wallowing. It was going to make a great show if I could ever get a shot on a big stag.

At times like this the pressures of TV can be immense, but I wouldn't trade my job for anything. Here we were, half way around the world, with production crews, the Outdoor Channel (who owned the show), families and outfitters all counting on me to make the shot and Dave to capture the action on film.

Even in the middle of a stalk, I can't help but sometimes think about such pressures. The key is turning those thoughts in to a positive, mental advantage. Rather than thinking, "I hope I don't blow it," I'm thinking, "I hope I get the chance to close the deal." This is when I often slip in a quick prayer.

Just as we broke over the edge of the ridge, into semi-open ground, Gerald came to an abrupt stop. He crouched, pointed downhill, then grabbed me. "One of the stags is coming right up the trail we're standing on," he urgently whispered.

Wasting no time, the three of us dove into the bush on the edge of the trail. "Get ready, he's very close," Gerald reaffirmed.

Nocking an arrow I glanced at Dave who gave me the nod, confirming he was ready to roll. No sooner had I got my release in the loop and I could see the top tines of the stag's rack, bobbing as he came up the trail.

Reaching full-draw before the stag's head became visible, I distinctly recall being mesmerized with how much antler he carried.

Caught off-guard, I was able to dive into the brush on trail's edge and reach full-draw just as a monster red stag came into view.

He was inside 25 yards, but quartering hard in my direction. I didn't like the angle, so held at full-draw.

The stag then crossed our tracks and grew nervous from the scent. He started trotting, still coming closer, then Gerald let out a grunt to stop him. The second the stag stopped, turned broadside and glanced our direction, my BowTech General quietly sent a Gold Tip Pro 400 arrow tipped with a 100 grain broadhead into the boiler room.

The shot came at 16 yards. Hugs of joy were exchanged, for at that single moment in time, the rewards of connecting on a shot and capturing the action for TV were unlike anything I'd ever experienced in the world of bowhunting. It's this heartfelt rush that drives me on each and every hunt.

The blood trail was simple to follow as it moved toward an open knoll. It was easy to see where the stag collapsed, then tumbled down a grassy ridge. He'd gone 50 yards, then fell and rolled downhill another 30 yards.

We could barely see the tips of his antlers sticking up above the tall, golden grass, now free of frost. Approaching the stag, Gerald gave me a pat of congratulations, then stopped me. Shaking my hand he offered, "You know what stag this is, don't you?" My face was blank. "It's the same stag that got away from us yesterday morning, the one that was in his bed and busted you."

I had no idea. I knew it was a big stag, but honestly, the shot happened so quickly I didn't even evaluate the rack before letting my arrow fly.

Approaching the fallen monarch, I was speechless by how massive the animal was, both in body and in antler. "He'll be over 500 pounds," shared Gerald. The stag carried 12 tines on each side of his rack, and his glistening red cape, I knew, would make for a beautiful mount that would let me relive this hunt for eternity.

That night, sleep came a bit easier, but the next few days we were back at it, hunting another red stag, prized sika deer and fallow deer. Those hunts were filmed for the TV show as well, but with a rifle. I love

It's monster red stags like this that attract hunters from around the world to New Zealand. This stag carried 24 total points.

bowhunting, but Game Chasers was largely backed by gun-affiliated sponsors at the time, thus the need to put those products to use.

With three days remaining, I'd planned on getting in some trophy trout fishing. Then Gerald approached me with a proposition. "If we can get you another red stag with a bow, would you be able to produce another TV show of the hunt?"

This is where the business side of hunting for TV has it's rewards, and pressures. I have a certain number of TV shows to produce each year, and Gerald recognized the value of having another hunt air whereby featuring Wildside Hunting Safaris. The idea is, viewers watch the show and if they like it, book a hunt. At this level it's business, and outfitters like Gerald recognize this and are willing to offer high-end animals. It works out well for everyone: the outfitter, myself and the viewers as it promotes the sport we all have a deep passion for.

One of hunting's most stunning big game animals, the regal red stag. This is an animal avid elk hunters will fall in love with.

I made a quick call back to the United States, to my good friend Tom Nelson. Tom is the longtime host of American Archer, a show I've made several guest-appearances on over the years. Tom is one of my favorite people in this business, and he was very interested in having us shoot a stag show for his program. The trout fishing would have to wait.

That afternoon found us sitting in a treestand. We saw some stags, but nothing passed close enough for a shot.

By daylight the next morning we were in another treestand, and animals were on the move. A fallow buck came under the stand first, but I didn't shoot. Then a pair of sika stags came out of the brush, about 100 yards to our right.

I love hunting sika deer as they remind me so much of the elusive Columbia blacktail deer I grew up hunting in Oregon. As the sika stags worked our direction, some red stags emerged from our left and also started walking our way.

Within minutes the biggest of the sika stags was inside 15 yard, feeding below the stand. He had no idea we were there. Because the red stags were slowly heading our direction we decided to pass on the sika. Later, Gerald would tell me that to his knowledge, at that point no one had ever arrowed a sika from a treestand in New Zealand. Had I known that, I would have shot him...the sika, not Gerald!

The group of stags we held-out for veered off the trail, never coming to within bow range. Throughout the rest of the day, into the evening and all through the next day, we'd have multiple stalks, but the animals weren't quite what we were looking for.

That night, sleep once again was tough to come by as roaring stags kept me awake. I wasn't complaining, as I can't think of a better reason to be kept awake.

On the final day of the hunt we awoke to another heavy frost. A good wind was in our face, so we covered ground, intent on closing the distance on roaring stags that could be heard bellowing in the distance.

The first stag we came upon was bedded in heavy brush, and sported an incredible drop-tine on the left side of his rack. Gerald had photos of this stag from several weeks prior, and I recall looking through his shots, wishing I could have a crack at that stag. My wish was becoming reality.

It took a long time, but I finally slipped to within bow range of the impressive stag who was still in his bed, facing away. I was above him and he had no idea I was near.

Reaching full-draw, my heart sank when I failed to find the stag in my peep. The sun was just cresting the horizon in front of me and I was blinded by the glare passing through my peep.

Squatting down to get beneath the incoming rays, I could now see through the peep, but the stag's vitals were obscured by brush. Forced to let down, when I did, the stag busted me.

He quickly gained his feet, but moved off slower than I expected. It took him a while to pass through the woods, out of sight, and when he did, I joined-up with Gerald. "That stag was limping a bit, eh?" Gerald quizzed. "I noticed that a few weeks ago when I saw him."

Not giving up on the drop-tine stag, we hoofed it around the timbered ridge he disappeared on. Slowly moving through the wet forest floor, as soon as we popped out of the timber, we found our lone stag, feeding amid tall grass. He was over 50 yards away, and the high grass coupled with my low elevation position made getting a shot impossible. I had no choice but to squirm closer.

At 36 yards the stag was finally clear and I confirmed the distance on the rangefinder. It was now or never. Bringing the General to full-draw, I anchored my 30 yard pin in the center of the stag's chest, tight behind his shoulder.

The Gold Tip arrow once again flew true, driving the Titanium 100 grain broadhead through the lungs in into the shoulder blade on the opposite side. He bolted over a knoll, coming to rest in a draw surrounded by thick, jungle-like foliage.

There was no ground shrinkage on that stag. In fact, his impressive drop-tine was even bigger than I'd thought. What did surprise me, however, was how much smaller the right side of his rack was in proportion to his left side. Also, his body appeared old and withered.

When skinning that stag we found where he'd taken a broadhead to the shoulder at least a year prior. The broadhead was stuck halfway through the right shoulder blade and had calcified formations all around it. That explained the stag's limp and lopsided headgear.

As our time in New Zealand came to a close, I felt satisfied, but melancholy. Not only was hunting the red stag roar a dream I never thought I'd get to experience, but I'd formed new friends I didn't want to leave.

Gerald Fluerty is one of the most genuine people I've ever met. His knowledge and passion for the outdoors and appreciation for the land

Gerald Fluerty and I were elated to tag this impressive red stag.
A massive drop-tine made him a truly unique animal.

and the wildlife is sincere. The deep love he has for his family is what life
is all about.

When I met Gerald, his eldest son, Ezra, a teenager, was soon to be
joining him as a full-time guide. I was fortunate to get to know Ezra and
hunt with him, too. He possessed the skills of his father, and at such a
young age, was sure to be a top New Zealand guide.

A short time after my hunt, Ezra's life was tragically taken in a car
accident. When I received word from Gerald, informing me of Ezra's
untimely death, tears flowed from my eyes. All I could think about were
my two sons...and how Ezra and his father got along so well and loved
spending time in the outdoors, together.

Meeting Ezra and Gerald immensely impacted my life. The Fluerty's
are a solid Christian family and knowing that when Ezra passed, he'd
be hearing red stags roar in the heavens, offered me solace. I hope to
one day return to New Zealand and hunt with Gerald, for he truly is a
special man, with a great family, living in a wonderful place.

Chapter 23:

Fallow Deer Down Under

*One never forgets their first big game animal taken with a bow.
For me, this was especially the case, as the hunt took place in
Australia, for a deer species I'd never before hunted.*

I started shooting a bow at a very young age. But by the time I was old enough to hunt big game, was tied-up with athletics which simply ate up too much time. As more friends started bowhunting deer, however, I felt the urge to make time.

It was then, my sophomore year in high school, that I suffered an injury that would keep me from pulling a bow for the next seven years. A year prior I was the second ranked javelin thrower among high school freshman in the country. I was getting invited to compete in some big events and was serious about this being my ticket to college. But plans soon changed.

While throwing on a cold day during my sophomore year, I tore and severely damaged several muscles in my right shoulder. Some of the damaged muscles extended all the way into my chest and I knew the moment it happened, it was serious. My javelin career was over.

The injuries forced me to change my throwing style for the remainder of my high school football years, where I was quarterback, going to a sidearm approach. I simply couldn't utilize those muscles over the top of my shoulder so had to improvise. It took years to regain my strength, both in a pulling (like a bow) and pushing (like bench press) motion.

When I finally picked up a bow again, it was in the mid 1990s. Technology wise much had changed in the bowhunting world during my absence. But I quickly learned and couldn't wait to finally hunt big game.

By this time Tiffany and I were living and teaching school in Sumatra, Indonesia. This was a great place to live for the simple fact Singapore was the hub city we flew in and out of. This meant we had many great and easy travel options at our fingertips. One place we love visiting–as it was so close to Sumatra–is Australia.

In all, I've hunted Australia four times, but my last trip, a 25 day do-it-yourself adventure, would be the first time I'd bowhunt the Land Down Under. I had intentions of doing more bowhunting on that trip, but things didn't quite work out as planned.

Because of the political turmoil Sumatra and all of Indonesia was facing at the time, I was advised not to take my bow out of the country, as I'd likely not get it back in. So, I arranged to meet a guy a few hours outside Sydney, Australia and borrow his bow. He assured me it had all the bells and whistles of the latest compound bow I'd been using, and he even had arrows to go with it.

When I arrived in Sydney, I drove to his house and we went into his garage. That was the first time he'd touched the bow in years. It was an old, rickety thing in need of serious attention. Waxing the string and checking the screws, all seemed in order, other than the fact it was missing a rest.

There was no bow shop in the little town, so I was on my own to fix things. Taking some bailing wire and electrical tape, I crafted a flipper-

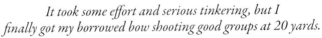

It took some effort and serious tinkering, but I finally got my borrowed bow shooting good groups at 20 yards.

like rest; it wasn't ideal but it worked. All but one of the sight pins had been busted off. There were other surprises, all minor compared to the rest and sight.

After getting things in order I was shooting the bow pretty good but didn't have near the effective range or the speed as what I'd been shooting with my bow back in Sumatra. I was kicking myself for not bringing my bow, but I knew I'd never see it again once the corrupt Indonesian custom officials got ahold of it.

Heading south, to the state of New South Wales, I figured pigs or goats would be the first animals I'd hunt as they are the most abundant in Australia. But I met up with a rancher who was more than willing to let me hunt his land, and he had fallow deer on it.

Fallow deer are not only Australia's, but the world's, most widespread deer species. I'd never hunted these deer before, and couldn't wait to get started. After getting some direction from the landowner, and advice as to where I could and should hunt, he turned me loose.

I love Australia and everything about hunting it. The people there are sincere and kind hearted. Knock on a door and before you know it you'll be having dinner with new friends. Every place I've ever visited, I've always been welcomed.

It took me a couple days to find my first fallow deer. When I finally laid eyes on a nice buck, his palmated antlers caught my attention. I'd seen fallow deer in zoos and game parks, and of course, plenty of photos of them, but to see one in the wild was even more awesome than I'd imagined.

As if the moose-like antlers weren't unique enough, his light brown coat covered in big white spots stood out against the dark brown brush near which he stood. He was over 400 yards away and had no idea I was around. Watching him through binoculars, his nervous, deliberate moves reminded me of a whitetail. It was mid-morning and with the winds being too shifty, I stayed back and observed the buck.

That evening I was back in the area and found the buck again. This time he was with two smaller bucks. I was able to slip within 100 yards of the trio of bachelors, but the two smaller bucks were between me and the buck I wanted, so again I was forced to be patient and not risk spooking them.

Eventually, the big buck separated from the other two and moved into a stand of very thick brush in the bottom of a dry creekbed. Figuring I could play the wind, and seeing how the ground was moist and quiet going, I felt I could get close enough for a shot. Slowly I worked down the creek bottom. Little did I know, but while I was moving down the buck was moving up the creek. The first time I saw him, he was 10 yards from me. He took a few more steps, coming to within five yards.

I sat motionless with no prayer of forcing an arrow through the tangled mass of vines. The buck never did see me, but he smelled me and busted out of there. I hiked back up the creek to a higher vantage point and glassed the area, but failed to find the big buck, or any buck, that evening.

The following morning I hiked to a high, rocky knob and was in position to glass the surrounding valley as a glowing sunrise broke on the horizon. I started where I'd last encountered the big buck, but saw no sign of him. Spotting a doe feeding in a distant meadow and a young buck working the edge of a brushy patch, there was no sign of a mature buck.

After nearly 30 minutes of glassing I was about to get up and move when a flash of white caught my eye. It wasn't 50 yards from me and at first I thought it was a kangaroo moving through the bush. A closer look revealed the spotted coat of a fallow deer. I knew it was a buck, but how big I couldn't tell through the thick brush.

Finally the buck fed into a small opening and I could see he was worth trying for. The wind was perfect, but I was in the open, not a good place from which to commence a stalk. I let him feed around the rocky knoll, then made a move to get in front of him. My hopes were that he'd keep feeding along the same line, eventually walking in front of me.

I kept the high ground and quietly moved toward where the buck was heading. I didn't see any sign of him. I knew he was either working his way back down the ridge or was beneath a rocky overhang which I couldn't see past. Figuring the buck was likely heading for the brush, I started to work my way down the hill.

As soon as I stood I saw the tops of palmated antlers bobbing as the buck fed below the rocky overhang. Slowly I crouched to my knees, arrow knocked. The buck was 35 yards out and if he kept moving along the same line, would walk right by.

When he fully emerged from behind the rocky ledge, I was shocked to see his nearly all white body with a dusting of light beige. He wasn't the same buck I'd seen feeding a few minutes prior; this one was bigger. This was the buck I'd gotten five yards from the evening prior.

At the angle he moved, the buck was slightly quartering to me and I didn't want to take that shot, not with the bow I was shooting. The wind was still good and the buck kept his head down while feeding as he walked along at a slow but steady pace. I waited and eventually the buck continued on his path of travel, giving me the perfect broadside shot.

Just as I was getting ready to draw, a second buck–the one I first laid eyes on–rounded the corner. Not wanting him to bust me, I drew while his head was down. As soon as I anchored the string in the corner of my mouth, the lead buck stopped and chewed on a mouth full of grass as he looked over the valley below.

Centering the only pin I had–which I'd sighted in at 30 yards–on the buck's chest, the aluminum arrow tipped with a 125 grain broadhead found the mark. I was surprised to see the arrow pass through the deer. In a flash the buck sprinted down the hill and into a thick tangle of brush.

Following the blood trail was easy and soon I found my first fallow deer–my first big game animal taken with a bow–piled-up in a heap of

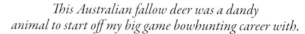

This Australian fallow deer was a dandy animal to start off my big game bowhunting career with.

Later in the hunt I arrowed this feral Merino ram. Merino wool is highly prized and after breeding, rams are routinely let loose to run free.

vines. Patience had paid off, and even today–years later–patience is my number one virtue in bowhunting.

At the time I didn't know all that much about fallow deer. The rancher said it was one of the biggest bucks he'd seen taken from that area. Later scoring would find him to be high in the bowhunting record books for fallow deer. I was both thankful and surprised that I got a second chance at this grand buck. I'll never forget approaching the downed fallow and how his heavy, palmated antlers glared under Australia's June winter sun. It was a rewarding sight.

I managed to arrow a Merino ram and a wild boar with that old bow before it fell apart on me. I also learned a great deal about bowhunting on this journey, mainly that I had a long way to go. But it was a starting point and proved to be the catalyst that got me hooked on archery. It was nice to be back in action after having been forced from bowhunting for so many years. Today, my shoulder is fully recovered and my bowhunting passion lives on. I can play catch with my boys and even throw a football with proper form.

Chapter 24:

Sumatran Jungle Adventures

Hunting amid a primary rainforest is one of the most challenging feats a bowhunter can face. Living in the middle of Sumatra, Indonesia, hunting in the dense jungle was my only option.

Fighting my way through overgrown, humid jungle, I couldn't get any closer to the rooting pigs. A chocolate brown stream on one side, a brush-choked hill on the other and tangled vines in my face, I was trapped. The commotion of the feeding swine 50 yards in the distance gave them away and I only had one option, to call.

Nestling into the buttressed root-system of a prodigious tree, I had a single shooting lane 10 yards long and three feet wide. Pursing my lips on the Jones Hog Call, I had no idea what to expect. I'd faced the rigors of jungle hunting for three months and never taken a boar with a bow, though was amongst pigs nearly every time out. But I'd never tried calling them, either.

At the muffled-echo of my guttural grunt, a pig immediately responded with a vibrant grunt that put mine to shame. Another call through the tube and brush and limbs were cracking as two pigs barreled my way. In seconds they were upon me and I was at full-draw, anticipating where they'd step. Stopping short of the shooting lane, I couldn't see them a mere 12 yards from me.

Letting down, I eased a soft grunt through the hog call, hoping to coax them into the shooting lane. The pigs responded and closed to six yards, but through the labyrinth of foliage I couldn't get a shot. I kept their interest for another minute or so, then they shuffled off.

Sumatra, Indonesia is home to a vast array of unique wildlife, and while big game is protected, pigs are another story. Various species of

During my time in Indonesia I encountered many wild Asian elephants in the jungle.

pigs abound in great numbers on many of the nation's equatorial islands and they can be hunted any time. Having never before hunted in a true jungle environment, I had a lot to learn.

In the dank, sultry jungle, sound doesn't carry far. This can have it's benefits as I've often heard pigs feeding and frolicking, giving me the window I needed to slip in, undetected. Taking advantage of their noisy antics allowed me to stalk fairly close, but the brush they occupy is usually too dense to thread a broadhead through. I soon realized I had to put the pigs where I wanted them if I ever hoped to get one.

With 10-foot long monitor lizards, civet cats and monkeys raiding bait stations before pigs could claim them, this popular method was out of the question. My only other option was to call them in.

I'd never before called jungle swine, and after a crash-course by good friend, Larry D. Jones on what methods he thought might work, I gave it a whirl. The first four out of five days I called, I drew in pigs. One whopping tusker would have tipped the scales to nearly 200 pounds, and stood almost waist high to a man. He approached within 10 feet of my calling site but with his incessant fidgeting in the tight brush, I couldn't finagle a clean shot.

Another time I moved in on a gang of rooting pigs in a swamp. The setup was ideal as a large, 15-foot opening sat between the pigs and I. My initial grunt got their attention, but they didn't budge. Another call, and all was still. Rustling dry leaves with my feet and giving out a high-pitch squeal on a predator call did the trick. Pigs often kill animals for food in the jungle and the sound of death sent them into a frenzy. A single pig skirted the opening and came right to me, but it was masked by saplings.

A few weeks later I worked a well-traveled trail paralleling a creek. The hog call worked it's magic and finally a young boar popped into the shooting lane. At barley 10 paces there was a small hole to shoot through, and my arrow made it. The chartreuse knock disappeared behind the front shoulder and the pig was instantly swallowed by jungle.

At last I had what I'd been searching for, my first jungle hog. Hunting a jungle environment is a great challenge and I had to adapt my ways to swing the odds in my favor. My ingredients for success were to find pigs working an area, move in as close as I could and begin calling.

There are two types of pigs on the island of Sumatra, the razorback type I was hunting and the giant bearded hog. I only ever saw one

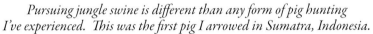

Pursuing jungle swine is different than any form of pig hunting I've experienced. This was the first pig I arrowed in Sumatra, Indonesia.

bearded pig, and couldn't get a shot. He stood well to my midsection and would have weighed in at over 300 pounds. The Eurasian pigs I sought averaged about 150 pounds, with a 200 pounder being rare.

Jungle hunting was the biggest test of my mental endurance that I'd ever faced. We lived a 1/2 mile from the equator, meaning every single day temperatures soared into the upper 90s. The humidity level was so high, sweat instantly flowed from my body the second I set foot outside.

The moist jungle held leeches that would drop on to my body from the trees above, or crawl up my pant leg if I sat in one spot for too long. Here, spiders grew large enough to catch small birds in their orbs, and ants measuring over an inch long were common. The lush, wet jungle is so rich in insect life that over 200 types of ants were once identified here in a single square meter.

The leaves of some plants were so big, I'd use a single leaf as a blind when calling. Tracks of the Sumatran tiger, tapir and elephant were often present. On numerous occasions I ran into elephants while hunting pigs, many of which I approached well within bow range of. I also saw the rare Sumatran tiger, a true spectacle to behold.

When I arrived on the island, I was contacted by an Indonesian gentleman whom the president of the country, President Suharto, appointed to organize and open the country to big game hunting. They wanted an American contact and I was it. They flew me to several amazing places, including the northern corner of Sumatra. It was here I got to hunt pigs, but also lay eyes on jungle habitat that few outsiders only dream of seeing. I saw all sorts of incredible animals, including the rare Sumatran orangutan. This species is highly overshadowed by

One of the most amazing spectacles I've ever witnessed in the wild; the rare Sumatran orangutan. These animals will likely become extinct within my lifetime.

the Borneo orangutan, simply due to media preference. It's very likely that the Sumatran orangutan will go extinct in my lifetime, and almost definitely before those in Borneo.

I walked the pristine land where a giant tsunami later wiped out Banda Aceh, the capital city of the Aceh province on the northern rim of Sumatra in 2005. I floated rivers in dugout canoes and set foot in areas no white man ever had, according to authorities. The sights I saw and the animals I observed, from the smallest of insects to the giant pachyderms, made for some very special moments. Water buffalo and banteng, axis, mouse and sambar deer, not to mention the rare Sumatran serow, an intriguing creature that looks like a cross between a Eurasian boar and a nilgai, are animals not many people get to see in their indigenous habitat.

Unfortunately, despite all our efforts, corruption and political strife prevented Indonesia from ever opening its doors to international big game hunting. President Suharto was voted out office, and though we were only one signature away from getting the green light, hunting in this great land never came to fruition, and likely never will.

In my four short years of living here, I saw primary jungles demolished to make way for palm oil plantations and rubber tree farms. With the vanishing jungles will go all the animals. It's sad that fellow hunters will never get the opportunity to see what I saw in this magical land.

Then again, the jungle is the toughest land I've ever set foot in. From overcoming the intense heat and humidity to dealing with numerous poison insects, snakes, scorpions and more, all of which I encountered every time out, is not for everyone. I guessed that hunters traveling to this land would be doing good to take one animal for every seven to 10 days of hunting, and that's with a rifle. The jungle is simply too dense to effectively hunt and it easily hides game.

One time I was called upon by the government to hunt down a man-eating tiger to the north of where we lived. The only way to approach this is with hounds and a rifle. Officials got me a gun and more than 30 houndsmen. The cat had killed a woman two days prior and was still hanging near the remote village.

The dogs did their part and found the cat. I was within 30 yards of the tiger for several minutes but neither I nor the men who were with me could ever see the cat which had bayed up on the thick jungle floor. Eventually the man-eater gave the dogs the slip and escaped without anyone seeing no more than its tracks and flailing tail.

Smaller than its Siberian cousin, the Sumatran tiger is a stunning animal to behold. I hunted a man-eater on the north end of the island of Sumatra, and though I was close, never got a shot at the beast.

Another animal I had an opportunity to hunt while living on Sumatra was the pigtail macaque monkey. Admittedly, this primate was never on my wish list, not until I had one too many close encounters with an aggressive male.

Hidden at jungle's edge, I patiently waited as a troop of macaques emerged into a small opening. With over 70 members in the troop, there was no mistaking, this was the group I'd been waiting for. Arrow nocked, I waited for the targeted male to emerge. The dominant leader in this tribe had earned a vicious reputation and local residents wanted him removed. After receiving a formal invitation from the local government to remove some of the over aggressive males, I knew exactly what needed to be done, and by law, I had to do it with a bow.

The Alfa male's aggression within this troop had raged out of control, for not only was he trying to rule a troop more than twice the ideal size, but he was now exuding his barbaric rulership on humans. No longer could people walk amongst the once docile monkeys. When any man, woman or child approached the troop, the big male was quick to attack.

People on foot, bicycles, mopeds and even automobile drivers reported being confronted by the insane beast. Weeks prior to our meeting at the jungle, he'd knocked and elderly woman from her bike and bit through her lower leg. A few days later he bit a chunk from a man's ankle as he escorted his young children home from school.

Capable of crushing a raw coconut with a single bite, adult pigtail macaques are stronger and faster than any man. Because troop numbers had grown unchecked and aggressive males were wreaking havoc on nearby residents. This is where I came in.

Pigtail macaque monkeys, like this
Alpha male, reeked havoc within the compound where we lived.
Their attacks on humans led to hunting opportunities I'd not anticipated.

Efforts to live trap the problematic monkey had proven fruitless for authorities, despite months of trying. Before they knew it, three problem male macaques thumped their chests as they maliciously aligned their troops. It wasn't until I was personally charged by one of these spiteful beasts that I learned just how threatening they can be.

Tiffany and I walked home from work one afternoon, where we served as teachers at an international school near the town of Pekanbaru. Like we'd done many times before, we paced through the troop, as human intrusion was of little concern. Before we knew it the dominant male tore around a bush and was in our face.

Not wanting to provoke an attack, we stood our ground rather than run. Full speed, he was at our feet in no time. Popping his fangs, his guttural growls found him a mere three feet from us before stopping. Hackles on end, he put his chest close to the ground. Back arched, head up, his dagger eyes pierced through us. We were defenseless.

I answered back with a loud shout and a wave of the arms. While my antics were less impressive than his, it kept him from sinking his teeth into one of us. But it's the possibilities of what could have been that rattled us, as Tiffany was six months pregnant at the time.

With over a half-dozen troops of pigtail macaques converging upon the little settlement in which we lived, conflicts continued to escalate. Dominant males sought control of larger troops and aggression reached catamount proportions. Broken legs, open wounds and infectious disease were now taking their toll on the monkeys, as rulers of the troops showed no mercy for those unwilling to abide by their rules.

I'd hunted man-eating lions and Nile crocodiles in Africa, and a man-eating polar bear in Alaska, so tracking down marauders of man was not a foreign concept to me. Over the course of the next few days, positively identifying the true problem animals was the goal. But once I nailed the biggest boss of them all, the rest nicely fell into place.

He had attacked another bicyclist the day prior to our final meeting, though I never imagined the ordeal ending in this manner. I envisioned sneaking up on him as he foraged for food, slipping an unsuspecting arrow his way. But as I watched for the troop to move from the jungle, a motorist drove by on a remote road. Erupting from the foliage the big male attacked the little truck, pounding on the doors and growling for all he was worth, and this with the car passing by at 15 miles per hour.

The monkey had no idea of my presence and when I let out a resounding woof, he wasted no time pinpointing my whereabouts. I came to full-draw while he covered the 50-yards in record time. His unorthodox gait kept me from holding my sight pins steady on his chest, despite the fact he was coming full-force, straight for me. When he stopped, his chiseled, 60-pounds of muscle five feet from me, I thought it was over for him.

But rather than pause, giving me an opportunity for a shot, in one motion he pivoted and was on his way back toward the jungle. Again I let out a woof, which caused him to pause for the brief moment I needed, 16 yards away. My broadhead flew true, passing through the beast. Tracking him in the hot, humid, bug-infested jungle was less than enjoyable, but when I found him piled beneath a giant tree, I knew there would be many happy people.

Authorities targeted two other problem males for removal, and once the big boy was gone, these two took center stage. They wasted no time filling his role, chasing people, threatening children and even burying their teeth into a few innocent souls.

Catching one of the males with his troop, his existence ended without him knowing I was around. The third monkey was elusive, but

One of three problem male macaques
I was requested to cull by local government officials.

Exploring a primary jungle is an awesome experience. I spent many days in this jungle, on the north end of Sumatra, surveying land and wildlife for possible international hunting opportunities.

when he slithered from his protected forest to nab a bait, he had no idea what hit him.

Word soon spread of the problem monkeys being put to rest. Children, who for months had been kept close to home, even within their confines, were free to once again play outside. Adults could let their guard down and enjoy outdoor activities that had been suppressed by the macaques. As for the troops of monkeys, they soon split into ideal sizes, each with it's dominant male to oversee their well being.

Confronting these animals on their home turf, where deadly vipers, venomous insects and stinging plants take their toll on the hunter, is unlike any form of predator hunting I've experienced. Coming face to face with razor-sharp fangs that have sliced through human flesh conveys a humbling aura. But the ultimate test lies in overcoming the fact that at any given moment, the hunter can become the hunted.

Being on constant alert for tigers, snakes or the tiniest of insects, kept me on full alert. Where malaria runs rampant, and where one mistake can mean your life, I never felt so mentally drained than after hunting the dense jungles of Sumatra.

Chapter 25:

Africa Lion Quest

I'd hunted Africa before, but this time was different. This time I was after lion, on the ground, spot-and-stalk!

As daylight broke, it was obvious I'd not be able to reach the ground blind. Between where I stood and the blind, glimpses of golden fur caught my eye as a lion slithered around the backside of a thorn bush covered in small, green leaves.

In the calm, crisp air of the southern Africa morning, the beast let out a roar that shook the earth. When the huge, blocky head of a golden-maned cat stepped around the bush, barely 500 yards away, there was no doubt I'd not be making it into the blind.

The 500-pound cat had no idea we were there, and my camera men, Dave Arabia and Jim Burnworth, kept rolling tape. As the big cat moved around the edge of the bush, ears laid back with a look of intensity in his yellow eyes, he let out another shattering roar. Silver steam rolled from his mouth, and saliva glistened as it dripped from his big, loose lips.

It's said that the roar of the African lion can be heard from over a mile away. I believe it, as I'd heard several lions up to this point in my life, but when it happens at such close range, it takes the game of bowhunting to a whole new level.

The afternoon prior, I'd taken a black wildebeest in the same area where we now faced the lion. Peter Tam, my PH (Professional Hunter), the trackers and I disemboweled the wildebeest then secured it a few feet up in a tree. Using stiff wire, rope and chains, we felt confident no lion could drag it off.

After securing the bait, we spent the next three hours chopping brush and grass, then crafting the ideal ground blind, complete with two shooting windows. Situated 30 yards from the bait, the intention

Two big, aggressive male lions kept us from entering our ground blind, and made the hunt very tense.

was to slip into the blind at first light, then wait for a lion to approach, hopefully giving us the perfect broadside shot.

When I asked my Peter why we didn't hike into the blind early in the morning, under the cover of darkness, he smiled, "Because there's a chance the cats might find it first." He was right.

Less than 20 yards from our roaring feline, another lion emerged from the brush. This cat came right out the pathway we'd carved into the blind. Had we tried entering the blind in the dark, there's a good chance I wouldn't be writing these words.

This second lion, also a male, stood, soaking in the morning sun which now broke over the horizon. Face covered in blood, belly bulging around the mid-section, it was obvious the big cat had fed throughout much of the night. Now he was moving into the bush, likely looking for a place to nap for the day.

On this hunt our target animal was a lioness. A big male lion was atop my bucket list, and had been since boyhood, but the lofty price tag that came with hunting them was out of mine and my producer, Jim Burnworth's, budget. Nonetheless, I felt blessed to be bowhunting any lion, and just because it was a female didn't make it any less of a thrilling experience.

The area I hunted had a healthy population of female cats, and Peter was keen on keeping their numbers in-check through the aid of hunting. A prized member of the Big Five, it doesn't matter if the cat is male or female. I'd taken two lions up to this point in my life, but those were with a rifle. Those cats were man-eaters, and a South Africa government official and I actually took four cats in one night, the last of which was killed at a charge, less than 10-feet from us.

Our objective on this hunt was to capture the action on film for the first series of African safaris to air on Adventures Abroad, a show I served as host of during its first season on the Outdoor Channel. Pulling off this hunt, with two big male lions in our midst, and no sign of a female, wasn't going to be easy.

Then, sudden movement in the bush out front and to the left caught our attention. It was what we were looking for–a lioness. She was over 100 yards away, but laid down under the overhanging limbs of a large thorn bush. Playing the wind, we wasted no time figuring out a way to reach her.

Though dry, the dirt was soft, muffling the sound of each step we took. In order to eliminate as much noise as possible, Dave stayed behind, filming from a distance, along with the tracker. Peter and I slowly moved forward, with Jim filming over my shoulder.

One male lion had moved into the heavy bush, away from us, while we lost sight of the other. Slipping slowly between bushes and small trees, it took us nearly 30 minutes to close the distance on the lioness, but we made it.

When we emerged from behind the last bush, we could see the head of the lioness, panting heavy with each breath. She was laying down, facing our direction, but had not seen us. Taking a reading with my rangefinder, it registered 45 yards. I felt confident at that range, but the angle wasn't right.

Moving a good distance to the right, we started circling around the lioness, looking for a clear broadside shot. The second we made it to the edge of a bush, the lioness laid her chin to the ground and pulled her ears back. It was a submissive posture and we soon learned why.

During the night, lions unexpectedly hit our wildebeest bait.

She still hadn't seen us, but the ominous presence of a big male lion sent her recoiling. It was obvious he didn't like her feasting on the bait, and let it be known.

He let out a monstrous roar then lunged at the lioness. Grabbing her by the back of the neck with his large, ivory fangs, he flung her over his back with seemingly no effort. Again he let out a roar of dominance, and again took her in his grasp and tossed her aside. Then his rippled, muscular body headed back towards the blind.

Not wanting to leave the cover of the bush, the lioness laid where she last landed. Fortunately, she was in good shooting position.

A final reading on my rangefinder registered 42 yards and I knew we weren't going to get any closer. With Jim filming over my right shoulder, Peter to my left clutching his big-bore rifle as backup, the time was now.

Bringing my BowTech Allegiance to full-draw, my nerves were on end. Knowing the male lion was close, I relied on Peter to keep an eye out for him while I focused on my target. The air was calm and all was quiet, and as I anchored the string into the corner of my mouth, I remember being shocked at how my peep moved with each beat of my heart. No question, being at full-draw on a member of the Big Five gave me a rush unlike anything I'd ever experienced.

Trying to calm the nerves, my index finger slowly pressured the release, sending a Gold Tip Pro 400 arrow on it's way. Moving at 333 feet-per-second from my 82 pound bow, the arrow found its mark, and the 100 grain broadhead did the job, slicing through the cat.

The lion winced at the shot, took one step and rolled over. Quickly nocking a second arrow, I didn't think I'd need it, not until the cat regained her feet. She staggered, then started stumbling right at us. Not wanting her to pick up steam, I let her have it with another arrow. This one, too, found the boiler room.

One of the biggest thrills of my bowhunting
life was taking this lion by way of spot-and-stalk.

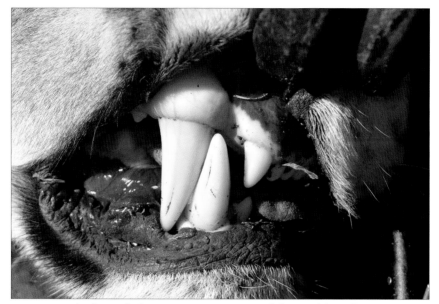

The fangs of a lion are an impressive tool designed for killing.

The cat went eight yards and expired. With the prized cat down, Peter began shouting and firing his rifle into the air in order to drive off the looming males.

Approaching the 300 pound cat, I was impressed at how lethal a bow can be on these, Africa's ultimate predator. After all, it's the lionesses who do the killing for the pride. Running my fingers over her thick canines, bulging jaw muscles and needle-sharp claws, I couldn't help but wonder how many animals she'd taken down in her lifetime.

Facing the king of beasts gave me a deeper appreciation for those hunters before me who had done the same. It especially gave me a heightened respect for the bushmen in the region who've hunted these cats for generations with little stick bows and frail arrows tipped with poison.

The taking of the grand cat marked a great beginning to this safari, one that would take me to three different regions where I'd end up arrowing 11 trophy-class animals, many of which qualified as top-10 in the record books. But Africa isn't so much about the record books. It's about the animals that attract hunters from around the world, whereby by allowing us the opportunity to experience the wonderful people and the captivating land, the likes of which are unmatched anywhere else on the planet.

Chapter 26:

Little Plains Game

Africa's game-rich environment offers hunters more variety of big game than anywhere on the planet. It's not uncommon to see 15 different species of game a day. On this safari, steenbuck, springbuck and bushbuck were what I had my sights set on.

After a lengthy stock through flat, open terrain, I finally got within bow range. Had it not been for the thorns on the low-growing bushes, I'd have thought I was hunting jackrabbits in the eastern part of my home state of Oregon. As it was, the antelope I pursued wasn't much bigger than a bunny.

The instant I reached full-draw, the dainty steenbuck darted behind a shrub, unaware of my presence. He was feeding and sticking close to a female. Steenbuck are often found in pairs, or the rams–as the males are called–on their own. They're not a herd animal as are so many of Africa's antelope species, which makes steenbuck a joy to stalk.

The first steenbuck I ever saw, 12 years prior in a different part of South Africa, I fell in love with. He was a good ram, about 20-inches tall at the shoulder, weighing all of 15-pounds with black, three-inch long horns jutting from the top of his reddish-brown head. He was a good trophy, but I never got a shot at him.

This time I yearned for the outcome to be different. As the ram I was struggling to get in my sights slipped behind some thick, tall brush, I let down. Arrow still nocked, I scurried around the brush in hopes of getting a shot. Now he was 22 yards out, but before I could find him in my peep, he was gone.

Not giving up, I snuck even closer this time and when I saw his red back moving amid yellow grass, I thought for certain I'd get a shot. He was inside 15 yards, but when I tried stopping him with a mouth squeal, he kicked into high gear rather than raising his head, pausing and looking back.

The last time I saw him he was 30 yards out and getting farther. He never did stop moving. Though I tried, I never could catch up with that monster ram.

By this time I'd moved a great distance from Armond Aucamp, my PH who stayed back to watch the action from atop a bald ridge. When I turned and started walking back, I saw Armond hop to his feet and start walking my way. Then he picked up the pace and began running.

Figuring he'd found another large steenbuck ram, I got excited and quickened my pace. When we met, Armond handed me a .22 magnum rifle. "If you don't want to go shoot that steenbuck, I will," he blurted out, breath short from running. "He'll be pushing six inches. He's one of the biggest steenbuck I've ever seen! Go get this ram with the rifle and we'll find you another to bowhunt."

Knowing I didn't have a prayer of catching up with the big ram with my bow, I swapped Armond for the gun and took off. It took me a while, but finally I got off a shot just over 100 yards out. Fortunately, the shot dropped the ram.

The dainty steenbuck is one of my favorite little antelope to pursue in Africa.

When I met up with Armond he couldn't get a tape on the horns fast enough. "Oh, man, look at this monster steenbuck!" Armond ordered. Both horns measured exactly 5 7/8-inches. Combined with their exceptional mass, had I taken this ram with a bow, he would have been the world record by exactly one-inch. I didn't know whether to mourn or shout for joy.

Reflecting on the four times I had the big ram at full-draw but couldn't get a shot, I pondered if there was something I could have done differently. Other than chance a questionable shot and risk crippling the ram, I couldn't think of anything–and taking an unethical shot was a decision I'm glad I didn't make, no matter how big he was.

The more I thought about it, however, the more dispirited I grew. When you think of taking an animal with roughly six-inch horns, and having him beat the current world record by an inch, that's like screwing up on a 550-inch bull elk. We're not talking a high fenced hunt here, this was all free-range, in some of the most open terrain southern Africa has to offer.

As we rambled down the dusty road, another glowing sunset lit the horizon ablaze in fiery orange. Africa's sunsets are the most stunning I've seen anywhere in the world. But when Armond slammed on the breaks and skidded to a stop, I immediately snapped out of my daze. Searching for a critter I assumed he tried missing with the truck, I saw nothing.

"Grab your bow, that's a giant steenbuck," Armond barked. I still had my release on, so quickly grabbed the bow and raced across the country road. "He went right over that little knoll, he should be right on the other side," instructed Armond.

Edging over the tiny hill, I caught glimpse of the ram moving away. Ranging a small opening I thought he'd enter, I got a 25-yard reading. Anchoring the string, I waited, holding on the opening. With a kill zone no larger than a tennis ball, I wanted to make sure all was right.

The second the ram reached the opening he stopped and I shot. Traveling fast, my Gold Tip arrow passed through his narrow chest as if it weren't even there. He went only a few yards and died.

Grabbing the stunning little ram, my steenbuck spirits were once again on high. Armond was thrilled when he saw me carrying my prize back to the rig. Again, he wasted no time slapping a tape measure to the ram.

"Congratulations Mr. Haugen," Armond grinned, extending his hand for a congratulatory shake. "You've just arrowed the new number 4 steenbuck in the world!"

This impressive steenbuck would have scored number four in the bowhunting record books had I chosen to enter him at the time.

It all happened so fast, I didn't have the adrenaline rush I usually experience. I knew he was a big ram, but not that big. I was excited as could be, then I thought to myself, "Man, if I could have closed the deal on that first ram, I'd have the number 1 and number 4 steenbuck in the world. My mind, as with most hunters, never stops thinking of what could have been.

In the end it didn't matter. Both rams are mounted in my den and each one holds very special meaning. That's all I ever ask for–fond memories to remind me of a great hunt with good people in God's stunning land. Their meat was delectable, too.

I was hunting the Karoo region of South Africa, near the famed Kimberly diamond mines. This land, rich in minerals, is a place that resembles more the moon than other parts of Africa. But due to the high mineral content in the seemingly lifeless soil, antelope species of many types grow exceptional headgear. Here live what many hunters consider to be the best steenbuck in all of Africa. This region of South Africa has claimed more record book rams than any other, and I was honored to experience it. The following day I'd get another steenbuck, though not nearly as big as the other two.

The steenbuck is an animal I never tire of hunting. Their big, black eyes, oversized ears and enchanting behavior make them one of my favorite antelope species to hunt in Africa. Whenever I'm on safari, I always inquire as to the region's steenbuck population, for they're one animal I can't get enough of.

The Karoo is also noted for it's big springbuck, among the largest on the Dark Continent. After having taken the steenbuck, my focus turned to springbuck. "I think we can get you a white springbuck with your bow, and maybe a common springbuck if we're lucky," offered Julian Theron, owner of Jules of The Karoo Safaris. "Tomorrow, you and Armond can hunt white springbuck."

Julian has built a life around managing the world's top springbuck. His passion for these magnificent antelope is contagious, and after spending a short time with Julian, learning from him about these cunning creatures, I was as excited to go on this hunt as any I'd been on. Julian and his lovely wife, Martisan, are two of the kindest people I've ever met. We have remained close friends since the first day we met.

The following day, Armond–Julian's top guide–and I were at it once again. This time we were in a ground blind, waiting for our quarry

*There's no problem spotting white springbuck;
getting close enough for a bow shot is another story.*

to come to us. Springbuck are nervous animals, always on the move, always on the lookout for danger. They hang in large herds, in vast, open sections of land, making stalking them with a bow a very time consuming, demanding feat, one many bowhunters and PHs consider close to impossible in this flat, open terrain.

After a few failed attempts at stalking, I knew why Julian and Armond had built the blinds from which to hunt springbuck. My time was running out and the fact we were filming these hunts for the Adventures Abroad TV show meant I had to try and take these animals in the fastest, most efficient way possible.

Into the blind we crawled, but it wasn't your normal hide (what the Africans call a blind). The 6x10-foot hide was dug three-feet deep into the red, hard, dirt, allowing me to stand and shoot at ground level. The front of the blind was faced with 6-inch diameter logs, and when adorned in grass and brush, made the perfect concealment. Three ideally shaped windows ensured I'd get a shot opportunity should an animal approach.

Before slipping into the blind we spotted a herd of white springbuck in the distance. Their white coats can be seen for miles, making them a fun and very different animal to hunt.

"There's a ram in there that would likely be the new world record," Armond pointed out. "In fact, there might be two." A year prior, Armond guided a bowhunting client to the new world record white springbuck, so he would know. In fact, that ram was taken from the same blind we were hunting in.

After about 45 minutes, a few young rams and some ewes came by, but nothing worth shooting. Minutes after they left, Armond spotted one of the two big rams. "They're heading this way," he whispered. Figuring they were close, I was crushed when I saw them 200 yards away, slowing their pace then bedding down.

An hour or so later another small herd moved our way. This one had a good ram in it but clearly it wasn't of the class the other two rams were, which were still bedded down.

"I think you should take him if he comes in," prodded Armond. "He's got exceptional mass and very heavy posts (the base of the horns) which should make up for his lack of length."

A few minutes later the herd was upon us. When the ram moved into range, I had to actually aim up at his vitals he was so close to the pit blind. The 15-yard shot was simple, taking out the ram's heart.

The Springbuck Man, Julian Theron, is deeply passionate about his springbuck. My white springbuck tied for the world record taken with a bow.

Approaching the stark-white springbuck, it was a beauty to behold, and stood out in stark contrast to the gray habitat in which he lived. "You're not going to believe this," Armond shouted. "I can't believe it myself!"

The ram's horns, though not overly long, were even more massive than we thought. As a result, he tied for the world record that was taken almost a year to the date prior. It was a total surprise to both of us, and a trophy I'll never forget. He was the first springbuck I'd ever taken, and spurred a love for my hunting this special antelope species.

The following day Armond and I were in another blind. This pit blind was identical to the first, though several miles to the west, near the base of some rolling hills. Our plan was to sit on a trail near a waterhole, intercepting common springbuck as they walked by.

The common springbuck subspecies is the mascot of South Africa's renowned rugby team. The beautiful antelope used to roam African deserts in herds numbering into the millions. Today, they are still one of Africa's most abundant antelope species, and they exist in four known subspecies: white, black, common and copper.

Jules of The Karoo Safaris is home to the world's largest springbuck. This massive common springbuck ram was later taken by a rifle hunter, and was the new world record by an impressive margin.

The common springbuck carries a dark chocolate stripe along the length of its midsection, separating a light brown upper-half from a white belly. They're a striking animal and one of the most widely recognized in all of Africa, if not the world.

Shortly after entering the blind we spotted a herd of nearly 20 common springbuck about 400 yards out. An hour later they were nearly within range. Moving into shooting position, I barely touched the top of the blind with my bow, but that was all it took. The herd couldn't get out of there fast enough, leaving nothing but a cloud of red dust looming in front of the blind.

Three hours later another herd approached. This time I was more careful. Of the more than a dozen head, only one ram was a shooter and I didn't want to blow it.

The hardest part was drawing my bow without being heard. There was no wind, and from inside the blind, every little sound was greatly magnified by the tin walls and ceiling. Finally, the fidgeting, always nervous springbuck ram turned his head to itch his offside shoulder. The moment his eyes disappeared behind his body, I drew.

The ground blind from which I arrowed a common springbuck.

As soon as he lifted his head and gave me the angle I was looking for, my BowTech Allegiance let loose, sending the arrow through the ram and into a thorn bush on the opposite side. Though he wasn't a giant ram, I didn't care. The fact I'd just arrowed a common springbuck was all that mattered to me, for there aren't a whole lot of these high-strung animals taken by bowhunters.

The more time I spent hunting small-statured antelope in Africa, the more I fell in love with them. But of all the little antelope I've bowhunted, my favorite is the bushbuck. While he's not exactly little–an average adult male weighs 100 pounds–they are much smaller than their larger spiral-horned cousins like the kudu and eland.

The common bushbuck is an elusive animal that reminds me more of blacktail deer, back home, than any other African animal. One of the most addicting animals to hunt in all of southern Africa, the bushbuck is shy, elusive, cagey and thrives in high numbers in the right habitat. These forest-dwelling antelope offer great thrills and endless fun.

"Over the generations my family has taken some very nice rams from this valley," shared new found friend, Guy Hockly, owner of Cullendale Safaris in the Cowie Valley. Stretching the tape over an 18-inch set of horns he held in his hands while chatting at his ranch, I could only dream of laying eyes on a bushbuck of this magnitude.

My common springbuck, one of the more challenging plains game animals to bowhunt in Africa.

It's these kind of horns that capture the attention of serious bushbuck hunters and why many regard the Cowie River Valley among the best of the best when it comes to hunting the prized Cape bushbuck. Situated in South Africa's East Cape Province, it's one of the most fertile valleys I've ever seen in this country. The bountiful water supply and densely wooded forests have allowed bushbuck to thrive here in mind-boggling numbers.

The later in the day it gets, the better the hunting for bushbuck becomes. If you're willing to sit in blinds and wait for the animals to come to you, this is one of the best ways to see numerous animals. If spot-and-stalk is your desire, then working river and creek bottoms, as well as forest fringes can payoff throughout the day.

Because bushbuck rely on heavy cover for protection during the day, slow hunts on foot can be made from early to mid-morning. The highest percentage hunt for archers, however, is sitting in a blind on the fringe of agricultural land late in the day. "They love to come feed on the green grass this time of year (winter)," noted Guy.

Being highly crepuscular, bushbuck hunting greatly improves as daylight fades. The first afternoon I sat in a blind, 16 bushbuck emerged from the forest and many within 75 yards, but none of the big rams came within bow range.

The next evening we relocated the blind a few hundred yards closer to the brushline from which the bushbuck were emerging. As the sun went behind the towering mountains on the west side of the valley, the woods came alive with barking bushbuck. It's a unique, unforgettable sound and the later it gets in the day, the more active the deer become.

Before long we had bushbuck passing by the blind. One little ram fed within six yards. Another ram, one I would have shot in a second

The bushbuck is one of the most addictive animals to hunt in all of Africa. They remind me so much of blacktail deer back home.

had it not been for the two rams farther behind him, came 23 yards from us. Things were looking up.

Before it was over 12 bushbuck came into the field before one of the two larger rams started feeding our way. Focused on him, I knew this was a ram worth taking. When he stood perfectly still and broadside at 42 yards, I gained a solid anchor-point and touched my release. The Gold Tip arrow passed right through him. The ram ran 30 yards, laid down and expired.

As Guy and I watched, one ram with horns well over 15 inches came out of the brush. Though he was out of range, he was a spectacle to behold. If there was one animal to bring me back to this valley, it would be the wily bushbuck.

My bushbuck carried horns 12 1/2" long and with his mass, would qualify as the new number 10 in the record books at the time. The thing about hunting bushbuck in this valley, you could rewrite the bowhunting record books at any moment. Every evening you're assured of seeing a top five ram, but the key, as with any bowhunting, is getting close enough for a shot.

The little antelope species of southern Africa are addicting to hunt. I've pursued these and other species in Namibia and Zimbabwe as well, and never tire of the joy and challenge they bring to bowhunting.

Chapter 27:

Glamour Plains Game Safari

When it comes to prized plains game in southern Africa, kudu top the list of most hunters. But the highly desired and once nearly extinct Bontebuck, along with the stunning scimitar horned oryx are two glamour species I never thought I'd get to hunt, until now.

After tagging my bushbuck with Guy Hockly at Cullendale Safaris in South Africa, it was time to put my bowhunting skills to the ultimate test. As you know by now, putting my name in the record book is not what drives me. Challenging hunts for big animals within any given species is what pushes me, along with the desire to share my thrills and encourage others to do the same.

I'm not a great bowhunter and don't pretend to be. But I love bowhunting more than any other form of hunting. When it's just me and the animal, my senses are taken to another level, one that makes me reach deep within myself to figure out what must be done to find success. Not only has bowhunting taught me a great deal about who I am, but it's pushed me to hone and further develop hunting skills I already had from many years of hunting with a rifle. The more we can learn about ourselves in the challenge of the hunt, the more proficient we'll become not only as a hunter, but as a person. That's what sets bowhunting apart from other forms of hunting.

When I took on the task of spot-and-stalk hunting for bontebuck, I must admit, I felt my chances of success were low. I'm an optimist, but also a realist and I know when the cards are stacked against me. I also know that with persistence and playing it smart, anything can happen in a hunt.

228   BOWHUNTING THE WEST & BEYOND

The bontebuck is an antelope that's indigenous to South Africa and makes its home amid some of the most open terrain in the country. They're a herd animal, meaning multiple sets of eyes are always on the lookout. Getting a rare bontebuck with a rifle is easy, for stalking to within 100, even 80 yards, is pretty straight forward. But sneaking within bow range is a whole different game.

At the time I committed to this hunt, the booking agent told me less than 10 bontebuck had ever been taken with a bow. He'd been booking hunts in South Africa for two decades, and though I never confirmed those numbers, they got my attention. Regardless of how many bontebuck had been taken by bow, it wasn't many and the hunt would be far from easy.

Due to their instincts to reside in the open and hang in large numbers, they were nearly shot to extinction. In the latter part of the 1800s, only 17 bontebuck remained in the wild. Once conservation efforts took root, bontebuck started to rebound. By the mid-1900s, hunting based organizations combined efforts and money which allowed the bontebuck to quickly flourish.

Because they live in grassland, nearly all the habitat bontebuck occupy is privately owned. Ranchers and farmers who were willing to set aside valued habitat for bontebuck reestablishment are largely to thank for the fact these animals are able to be hunted today.

One of these men was Guy Hockly's father. In fact, I was one of the first to ever bowhunt the land on which the bontebuck roamed in the heart of where Guy's father helped get them reestablished. The fact they'd not been hunted much at all, and never by a bowhunter on this 25,000 acre block of land, left me more optimistic.

With several herds numbering close to 100 head, finding bontebuck was easy in the grassy lowlands of the Cowie Valley. However, with so many eyeballs in the vast, open terrain, getting to within bow range was going to be a challenge.

The first few stalks found me within 80 yards of three different herds but they all busted me. Knowing I'd have to try and catch the bontebuck moving near what few bushes pocked the land, I knew that wasn't going to be easy.

As the afternoon heated up, herds of bontebuck began to move high on to a distant escarpment across the valley. Seeing how there were some tall bushes scattered around in the bottom and slightly up the ridge, I felt there was a good chance of using this cover to get within range.

Very few bontebuck have been taken with a bow. With so many eyes, in such open terrain, stalking within range of a trophy ram is one of bowhunting's ultimate challenges.

Guy and I spotted a good herd of bachelor rams but it took us a while to reach them. By the time we got there they were up and walking. But they were moving back down the hill, to graze on the valley floor. Scurrying as quickly as we could, we made it to the last row of bushes that separated the grassland from the rocky escarpment. There, we waited.

When the first ram passed by at 70 yards, we knew the rest of the herd would follow. There was no wind, and with my BowTech Allegiance rocketing arrows at 333 feet per second, I knew I could make the shot. I'd been shooting good all summer, practicing regularly at 80, 90 and 100 yards. I like long distance practicing and though most of the animals I've taken over the years have come within 40 yards, my effective range has held pretty constant at 70 yards. That's not outlandish for many hunters where I'm from, out West. When it comes to long-range shooting on animals, it's not my ability which I last question in my mind, rather the behavior of the animal I'm about to shoot.

"The last ram in the group is the biggest," whispered Guy. "He'll follow the exact same path as those ahead of him, so be ready. If he stops, go ahead and have a go."

Generally, bontebuck are an animal that follow those in front. If the lead animal stops, they all stop. If the lead animal moves at a quickened pace, they all do. So when the herd began to slow, then stopped as my target ram approached a narrow shooting lane, I knew I was going to get a chance.

One final ranging confirmed 72 yards. But the moment I released the arrow, the herd started moving, and I struck the ram a bit back. We watched the herd for a while, then saw the hit ram peel-off and bed down. We gave him time.

Stalking in to finish off the ram, he jumped up and ran off. Again, we gave him time, but again he bolted before I could get another arrow in him. We watched him hobble around a ridge, out of sight, and decided to give him more time.

After nearly 30 minutes of waiting, we heard a rifle shot come from around the ridge. We hustled to the top to find Guy's partner and his client a few hundred yards away. We figured they'd shot a black wildebeest, but when they called us on the radio, saying they'd finished off my bontebuck, my heart sank.

Actually, the rifle shot was high on the ram's back, and it ran down into some brush on the valley floor. We finally located the ram, standing on the edge of some shrubs. After a lengthy stalk, I got to within 20 yards of the still standing ram and put a final arrow in him.

It was a bitter-sweet moment, for I'm confident I could have finished off the ram with my bow, but it was also good to have the ordeal over with. The rifle hunters had no idea where we were, and couldn't reach us on the radio when we were around the ridge. They made a call based on what they observed with a wounded animal and there was nothing I could do about it now. I would have likely done the same thing.

For me, the hard part to swallow was the fact that gorgeous ram would have been the biggest ever taken with a bow. A world record of a species few men have ever taken with a bow; that's what drove me on this hunt. Guy wasn't overly pleased, either, and right there we decided to try for another ram the following day.

Three days later we were still trying. Rarely was there a moment when we weren't either stalking bontebuck or planning a stalk on them. The animals were everywhere, it's just that they were incredibly tough to get close to. If they didn't bust us with their acute eyesight—always

The Cowie Valley is truly unique to this part of South Africa, and is home to a variety of plains game species.

on the search for predators–then they smelled us in the swirling winds which whipped around the valley.

We pretty much stuck to stalking bedded animals, as often times they spread out when laying down. Trying to single-out a ram was our goal, and finally, after several failed attempts we caught a break.

We watched a herd of rams walk a couple hundred yards up an escarpment and bed amongst a smattering of high growing bushes. Though it was winter, the bushes still had leaves on them in this mild climate. That offered us just enough cover to make the stalk we'd been working so hard for.

Hiking up a ridgeline, out of sight from the bedded bontebuck herd, our plan was to come down on them from above. The biggest ram was bedded below and to the right of several others, and though I wanted him in the worst way, I knew it wasn't possible.

Instead, I took the best opportunity given, focusing on one ram that was bedded a good 10 yards above all the others and closest to me. The wind was perfect but the going slow. It took more than 30 minutes to cover 150 yards and I had to select a route very carefully, making sure there was always brush between the ram and us.

By this point it was just my camera man, Dave Arabia, and I. Guy stayed back, watching the action from the ridge top. Not only did we

232

This bontebuck would have gone number four in the world with a bow. PH, Guy Hockly, is a hard-working, very knowledgeable man I love hunting with.

have to worry about spooking our target ram, but any bontebuck, for if one blew, they'd all blow.

Finally, picking a hole in the brush I ranged the back of the ram's head at 30 yards. At the same time I drew the bow and moved to my left for a clear shot, Dave moved with me, hefty camera on his shoulder. But there was a bush I failed to see, and I had no shooting lane. No matter how hard I tried, there was just no getting an arrow to the ram from my position.

Quietly we backed out and came in from a different angle. This time the ram was 32 yards out, but I couldn't get a shot from that angle, either. We'd have to wait for him to stand.

Amazingly, the very moment I nocked an arrow, the ram got up, stretched and just stood there. It was a hard quartering away angle, but I knew I could make it. Running the broadhead in behind the last rib, I got instant, solid penetration.

Now the whole herd was up and running. Right back into the bottom of the valley they headed, where they always do when threatened. Fortunately, our ram didn't make it that far.

The ram was bigger than I thought, though not as big as many we'd seen over the past few days. Still, he taped out at what would have been the fourth largest bontebuck ever taken with a bow at the time, and that was more than I could ask for.

I was the first hunter to ever take a bontebuck on this piece of land in the Cowie Valley, though I won't be the last. It's now revered as the best piece of real estate to hunt bontebuck in all of South Africa, and I believe it. I also believe the record books will be written and rewritten from this magical land.

From where I took that bontebuck, we could look across the flats and see black wildebeest, blesbuck, springbuck and zebra. Higher in the hills, waterbuck and kudu, along with eland and nyala, could be seen. In fact, the next day we'd be hunting kudu in those hills.

The habitat in which the kudu lived in this valley was very dense forest, reminding me of where I grew up hunting Roosevelt elk. Compared to other places I'd chased kudu, this area was unlike anything I'd seen.

It didn't take long to reach the conclusion I'd need to spend several days in this thick, rugged terrain if I wanted to nail a kudu with my bow. Then Guy brought up the idea of hunting from a blind. "I have a hide (blind) built up in the hills, where kudu move along a trail between feeding and bedding areas. I think we should give it a go."

Figuring I'd be entering into a tiny ground blind, I was shocked to see a brick blind large enough to accommodate six people, complete with mortar, multiple windows and a carpet to keep things quiet. Most PHs I've hunted with in Africa are serious and do things right or don't do them at all. That's one reason I love hunting with these folks so much; they are as hard-core as it gets, especially Guy Hockly.

Guy was right, for in the last hour of light on our first afternoon of sitting in the blind, the hillside came alive with kudu. First cows and calves passed then two nice bulls materialized from nowhere. They browsed, heads in the trees as they slowly moved our way. Because of the brush, I was nervous as to whether or not I'd be able to pull-off a shot.

Then one bull stepped clear and stood still, broadside. The 20 yard shot found my 100 grain broadhead piercing both lungs, and after traveling barely 50 yards, the bull collapsed. He was a nice East Cape kudu, and though not nearly as large as their Southern Greater kudu cousin, he would have scored as the new number six in the world for archery. It was a fitting end to one of my most memorable safaris, and I hope to one day return to the magical Cowie Valley.

The most talented camera man/editor I've ever worked with, Dave Arabia, and I have shared many special moments over the years. This is one of my favorite shots, celebrating a top-10 East Cape kudu taken for the Adventures Abroad TV show.

Like the bontebuck, the scimitar horned oryx was an animal I'd always dreamed of one day hunting but figured I'd never get the chance. That all changed when I hooked up with Peter Tam, of Tam's Safaris. I'd taken lion and rhino with the Tams, and it was also here that I laid eyes on my very first scimitar horned oryx. They are a very striking animal to see in person, and Peter sensed my desire to hunt one.

Traditionally, the scimitar horned oryx once roamed such northern African countries as Chad, Senegal, Niger, Sudan and Egypt, and thrived in the Sahara Desert. Today, hunting opportunities exist only on private lands where herds have been introduced and are well managed.

Considered by many to be the pinnacle of Africa's plains game, the scimitar horned oryx carries a gorgeous pelage. Both sexes carry the long, black, curving horns, an impressive sight even from a distance. As with members of the oryx family, the horns of a mature bull are more massive though not as long as those of the adult cows.

Though their white coat is designed to reflect solar rays, perhaps the most interesting biological adaptation of the scimitar-horned oryx to it's intensely hot, dry indigenous habitat, is its ability to raise its body temperature. When there is a shortage of water, these animals are

One of the world's most striking antelope species, the scimitar horned oryx can only be hunted in limited places.

reportedly able to raise their body temperature to 116° Fahrenheit in order to avoid sweating, whereby conserving water.

Capable of tipping the scales to more than 400 pounds, these oryx depend mostly on grass, herbs and roots. Their original habitat was arid, even rocky terrain and sometimes thick brush. Today, thanks to their propensity to adapt, the oryx survives well in the food-rich habitats they've been introduced to.

Capable of living up to 20 years in the wild, historically herds of these animals numbered into the hundreds. Family units may also make up a herd, and when not rutting, bulls may go off on their own or form small bachelor groups. That's exactly what happened with the bull we found; he was a loner.

We spotted him across a valley, bedded on the south-facing side of a large ridge. It was mid-morning, and given his position, we'd have to hike around the ridge and come at him from behind.

Deciding to go for it, Peter felt confident that given the conditions and the bull's position, we could get within bow range. I agreed. Getting into range was one thing, getting off a shot in the high winds was another. That would be a call I'd have to make when the time came.

Well into the stalk and crouched against the side of the mountain, I questioned whether or not we should abandon our efforts. We were nearly two hours in to the stalk, but getting closer. However, 40 mile per hour winds pounded us and the even more intense gusts would make it near impossible to hold my bow steady.

Given the conditions, we decided to get aggressive and wasted no time closing the distance. The high winds did mask our footsteps on the hard, African soil, allowing us to move quickly. The bull was bedded on the backside of a knoll and our only hope of getting to within range would be to try and slip in from directly behind him.

Because the bull was bedded on the side of a ridge, he remained out of sight for most of our stalk. In fact, not until we got within 60 yards did we finally catch a glimpse of his horns. Fortunately, he was still in the same place, laying down, facing straight away.

Once we broke the 50-yard barrier, I felt good about closing the deal. At this point we'd made it to the inside edge of the same little bowl the bull was bedded in. The wind was not howling quite so intensely here, but it was still strong enough to cover our noise.

As we inched to within 40 yards, my optimism dropped. It wasn't until this moment I discovered that, though the bull was still facing away from us, his front end was considerably lower than his hind quarters. This meant the only thing I had a shot at was his tail, and that's not a shot I felt comfortable taking in this situation.

Slowly I crept forward, Peter directly behind me. We made it to 37-yards, then 35, then 32. At this point I could see the entire bull, his chest cavity rising and falling with each breath. It was obvious he wasn't sleeping, but at the same time, he wasn't intently surveying

Thorns are just one obstacle hunters must contend with while in Africa.

his surroundings, either. He seemed content in his old, beaten body, obviously on the downhill cycle of his life.

Arrow knocked, I sat back on my heels, knees and toes buried in the dirt, waiting for the bull to stand. Then his left ear twitched, followed by a quick pivoting of his right ear. Instantly his nose went into the air and that's when I felt the wind slap the back of my neck. He smelled us.

Coming to full-draw I knew what was next. All I could hope for was that as the bull stood, he'd give me a chance to let my lightening-quick BowTech do its job. That didn't happen.

As fast as the bull stood, he was on an all-out sprint, straight away. Tracking him with my sight pins, I prayed he'd stop. Through his rangefinder, Peter was spouting off distances as the bull got further from us. "Forty, 45, 50 yards now," Peter barked. Then the bull stopped and cocked his head back to see where the smell had come from.

Still at full-draw, I didn't have a shot. Then the bull turned sideways and looked back. "Seventy-two yards," Peter announced. We were between wind gusts and as I touched my release, the Gold Tip arrow was on the way. Watching the white fletches bury behind the right shoulder of the magnificent bull was an image that will forever remain

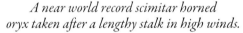

A near world record scimitar horned
oryx taken after a lengthy stalk in high winds.

Africa's most famous tree, the baobab.

etched in my memory bank. I couldn't have walked up and placed the arrow any better. How I did it, I don't know.

Dropping into a brushy ravine, we followed the hit bull. Though it wasn't necessary, I gave him an insurance shot and he was down for good. Oryx are among the toughest plains game in Africa and I didn't want to chance it.

Running my hands over the bull's reddish coat, gripping his massive, sweeping horns and admiring such a breathtaking trophy is a moment I never thought I'd get the luxury of experiencing. I've been blessed to hunt numerous African animals, but this one for a prized scimitar horned oryx, a bull that scored as the third largest ever taken with a bow, goes down as one of the most memorable.

Chapter 28:

World Record Rhino

Africa's Big Five are what many hunters dream of pursuing. On this hunt for white rhino, I cranked my poundage down, screwed a dart on to the end of my arrow, then delved in to one of the most hair-raising hunts of my life.

There I stood at full-draw, 22 yards from one of the world's largest mammals. The bull white rhino was bedded down, but the cover was so dense, there was no way of threading an arrow through the thornbush. After holding more than a minute at full-draw, I let down and waited.

Searching for a hole in the bush, we inched closer. Inside 15 yards there was still no opening. The bull had no idea we were near, his giant nostrils flaring and contracting with each breath. He was calm, then the wind changed.

Nimble as a cat, the bull stood, pegged us, and tore off through thorns so thick, a human would never have never made it. Fortunately he went in the opposite direction, which slightly eased the pain of having blown a stalk on the giant beast.

There's no such thing as a small rhino, and given our close proximity to the bull, he seemed exceptionally huge. Two big horns, a body weighing nearly four tons and a beady-eyed grimace that sent chills down my spine, he left no room for error, especially since we were hunting with a bow set at 28 pounds.

I was with Professional Hunter, Peter Tam of Tam Safaris in South Africa's East Cape Province. The Tams are world-renowned as the premier outfitters of white rhino, as they've been managing and hunting them for years. The land is pristine, basic to navigate and is designed for spot-and-stalk bowhunting rhinos.

Glassing from elevated hillsides, spotting a rhino in the valley below is how these hunts typically commence. From there, wind direction is evaluated and a plan of attack made. At first glance it seems like a slam-dunk hunt but the closer you get to these giants the tougher the odds of connecting become.

The hunt grows most tense when within 50 yards of a bull, where visibility greatly diminishes amid thick brush and the chance of a charge rises. The thick maze of white thornbush where these rhinos prefer bedding, creates a curtain that can be impenetrable to see and shoot through. Blending in so well with the thorns, even seeing a rhino at close-range becomes a challenge in this habitat.

"We must be very patient and pay close attention to the wind when closing in for the shot," advised Peter. "These animals have a nose unlike anything and their hearing is very keen, as well. If one does turn on us, wait until the last minute before diving out of the way."

A charging rhino picks up speed surprisingly fast, as I learned from personal experience on my first African safari, in 1995. "The biggest mistake people make is turning and running the moment a charge begins," continued Peter. "Instead, let the rhino get lined out and build up speed. Once he gets moving in a straight line, it's hard for him to turn. Don't even try to outrun one, for they are too fast for humans. Wait until he's about three yards from you then bolt to the side as quickly as possible. Once he's by you, stay still, for he'll likely keep running, and once he loses sight of you, you're safe."

Shortly after the first blown stalk, we were searching for another bull. Peter located a fresh pile of droppings on a frequently used territorial post and felt the bull wasn't far. Slithering around through the bush proved futile, so we moved to high ground to glass. It didn't take long to locate the bull, standing near where we'd just been walking.

Planning a stalk, Peter felt confident we could get on this bull if he held in the same place. Snaking our way down the hill and into the flatland, we were soon within 100 yards of where we'd last seen him.

"Let's take off our shoes so we can move quietly," Peter suggested. The stalk was intense, as I spent as much time staring at the ground, tiptoeing around fallen, four-inch long thorns, as I did searching for the rhino.

"There he is," whispered Peter. "See his foot under that thornbush? He's moving! Get ready, he should walk out into that opening. It's less than 30 yards."

Timing the bull's pace, I drew before he hit the opening. Anchored, I felt steady, until the bull turned and faced us just as he reached the edge of the shooting lane. "I don't have a shot," I whispered to Peter. The bull stood, testing the wind.

His magnum-sized nostrils pumped hard as he tried pinpointing our locale. Still as could be, we dared not move for fear of a close-range charge. Pivoting his ears like radar antennas, the bull worked hard to figure out what was out of place in his domain. The standoff lasted nearly a minute before he grew nervous and busted out of there.

Had I been shooting a broadhead, the hunt would have been over. On this hunt, however, I was using a specially designed dart, one which required getting extremely close and hitting the right spot. The dart contained 2 milliliters of tranquilizing potion that would put the rhino down for 15 minutes. Darting a rhino with a bow is something new to South Africa, darting them, in general, is not.

For several years the South African Department of Nature Conservation has been darting white rhinos in order to monitor their health and help deter poaching. In 1990 the first sport hunter darted a rhino with a rifle, and paid money to do so. Today, darted hunts are very popular among sportsmen and highly beneficial to both the hunting and conservation of the species.

The white rhino is one of hunting's greatest conservation success stories.

242

Over the years, hunters and the money they have spent to dart white rhinos are the main reason these animals have bounced back from the brink of extinction. On a global scale, it could be the most powerful testimony there is of hunters serving as leading conservationists.

It takes a white rhino bull about 20 years to reach full maturity, and many outfitters don't like killing bulls until they are closer to 30 years of age. This allows the dominant bulls to pass on their genes and carry out a full life while naturally perpetuating the species. White rhino populations are very stable and, in fact, doing better than ever in many of their historical ranges of South Africa. Their thriving success is largely due to darted hunts.

To kill a white rhino demands big dollars–about $100,000 as of this writing–and there are plenty of people willing to pay it. However, for much less money a bull can be darted, either with gun or bow, and hunters still get to enter the score in the Safari Club International record book. The length and girth of both horns are added together to get the overall numbers used in the book.

However, this catch-and-release style of hunting, often referred to as a "green hunt," has many sportsmen and hunting organizations on edge, fearing it fuels the fire for the anti-hunting groups. In reality, that's not the case.

Truth is, there are very few animals in the world that can be darted in this way, based on the simple fact they would be impossible to recover in a timely manner and administer the anecdote to. There are no animals in North America that could be darted and consistently recovered. Even in Africa, there's no catching up to the many antelope species, or even the big cats, once darted. Elephants are so huge, the impact of their collapsing from a sedated dart could force them to hemorrhage internally and die.

There's no mystery in hunting the white rhino. They are grazers and live in low elevation farmland that is easy to access. Nature Conservation officials and land owners know the areas where all the white rhinos live, as they are closely monitored against poachers. Some of the biggest bulls in the world actually have guards watching and traveling with them through the wild, 24 hours a day, 365 days a year. Their horns are in that high of demand on the black market and they are much more valuable to the country and its economy if kept alive within game viewing parks.

It's worth noting that each rhino is darted only once every year or two at the Tams. Only when blood and tissue samples are needed to monitor their health are the rhinos darted. That was typically costing the Department of Nature Conservation about $1,500 per animal to carry out. Today, hunters are paying over $10,000 to dart a rhino, and a large percentage of that money goes right back in to managing the animals.

Some people believe that the same rhino is darted multiple times each year, and that's simply not the case, not here. In fact, on these darted hunts, a trained Conservation officer tags along, overseeing the activities. He is the one who performs all the testing on the animal and also carries anecdotes for the rhino and the humans involved. One drop of the poison is so potent it would kill a human in a few minutes. There is no room for a mistake.

On this hunt I was shooting a specially built bow with a draw weight of only 28 pounds. My normal hunting bow, a BowTech Allegiance, was set at 82 pounds and was throwing arrows 333 feet per second–a significant difference to say the least. My rhino bow, a BowTech Miranda, had lightweight limbs installed so as not to risk shooting through the rhino's skin, causing unwanted damage. The dart, which Peter himself designed, screwed directly into the insert and it took only a few test shots to get the setup sighted in and ready to rock.

Later on the morning of my hunt, one of the trackers spied what seemed to be an exceptional bull. The tracker used a horse to gain high

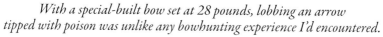

With a special-built bow set at 28 pounds, lobbing an arrow tipped with poison was unlike any bowhunting experience I'd encountered.

ground and from this vantage point could see a bull move into cover for the day. By the time Peter and I arrived, the bull had his backside buried tight against a wall of thorn trees, but was still standing.

We were 200 yards from the bull and he had no clue we were near. "Watch, he's going to bed down right there," pointed Peter. No sooner had the words passed his lips when the bull swayed his head to one side, then the other, sniffed the air and plopped his massive body right where Peter said he would. It came as a comfort to me, knowing I was with a PH who was so tuned-in to rhino behavior.

Slipping off our shoes, we discussed a plan of attack. It appeared we'd be able to walk straight into the slight breeze, using one of two thornbushes for cover. Nearly an hour later we were within 40 yards of the sleeping giant, but too much brush prevented my slipping an arrow into his shoulder. We had no choice but to back out and approach from a different angle.

Thirty minutes and several thorns-in-the-feet later, we were within 40 yards, once again. This time all felt right, and I prayed the crosswind would not change and ruin our third stalk of the day. Slowly we edged closer, using a dirt trail to mask our sound and brush to conceal our movement.

Throughout the rhino stalk, dealing with giant thorns in our socked feet was common.

At 30 paces Peter ranged the bull, then stepped aside to allow me to reach full-draw. Anchoring the string, I rested the 30 yard pin on the rhino's right shoulder. But an overhanging branch, one I feared would send my arrow off-course, hung in the way. Slowly I moved to avoid the branch, and as I did, the rhino stood, alert.

His massive body towered above the brush and at such close range, it seemed like I had to adjust and shoot up at him. His fearless face stared straight down my arrow shaft, through my sights, past my peep and dead into my eyes.

Regaining my composure, I was able to settle the 30 yard pin on his massive shoulder. The Gold Tip Ultralight Pro 400 arrow tipped with the dart–not the usual broadhead–was on it's way. The instant I released I thought I'd blown it. The arrow was sailing a good three feet over the bull's back. "Great, I just missed an animal the size of my truck," I thought.

The arrow arched so high and moved so slow toward the bull, I actually had time to ponder how I could have missed at such close range. Then it started losing elevation...fast. As the heavy arrow dropped, the dart buried into the center of the bull's shoulder. A direct hit!

The bull exited the brush on the same trail we stood on, but fortunately in the opposite direction. Within 10 minutes the bull was down, prone on locked front legs, comfortably sitting on his hind-end. With the sedated bull relaxed, Peter, the biologist and his team went to work. First and foremost was monitoring the bull's safety; applying eye-drops, covering his eyes and stuffing cotton in his ears to calm his senses. Then the biologist stepped in, taking blood and tissue samples and recording other valuable data to be used in helping monitor the overall health of the bull. Next, a microchip was implanted into the bull's horn to track it down should poachers strike. Last, the rhino was doused with water to keep him cool. In less than 15 minutes the work was complete, the anecdote administered and the bull sent on his way.

Reflecting on my approach of the downed rhino, I was taken by his immense size. His nose was as wide as my torso, his nearly 30-inch long front horn had a circumference that almost equaled my waist size, 34-inches. Taping out both horns, he scored 99 1/2 inches, making him the new pending world record under the darted category with a bow in the SCI record book. He would have shattered the world record bull killed with a bow, which made the experience even more special.

While snapping some photos I nudged into the side of the sedated bull. I could feel the chest of the conscious bull expand, touching my

The world's largest white rhino ever darted with a bow. Tests were performed on the massive beast and he was soon released to roam the savanna.

back, with each breath. "If he falls on me, there's no way these guys are getting him off," I thought. So I moved around to the front, by his nose. It was much better getting snot blown on me than bearing the thought of being crushed by this monster.

I would have been pleased with any rhino on this dream hunt, but to come away with an animal of this magnitude surpassed my wildest dreams. I never did enter him in to the record books, something I've never done with any animal. Personally, for me, the hunt is about the animal, not seeing my name in print.

My greatest reward came in watching the bull walk off, a feeling I'd never experienced as a hunter. Knowing hunters' dollars have literally saved the white rhino from extinction, and that I was able to have a small hand in it, was all the gratification I needed.

Closing Thoughts

In my short lived bowhunting career–about 15 years up to this point–I've been blessed to go on many exciting hunts. I have TV and writing to thank for that, for if I wasn't making a full-time living at this, there's no way I could have afforded many of the hunts you've just read about.

For me, bowhunting is a sport where the learning never stops. However, because I've been able to go on so many hunts in such a short time, my learning curve has been greatly expedited. When hosting BowTech's TV show and Adventures Abroad, for example, I was going on more than 30 hunts a year. With so much time spent in the field, I learned a lot, fast.

There are several hunts I didn't include within these pages due to the simple lack of space. Some were successful hunts, some not, but I always came away with more knowledge.

There's the hunt for Illinois whitetail where I arrowed my first buck from a treestand; he wasn't a whopper, but I'll never forget that hunt. There's the time a bear crawled up our treestand in Alberta; we took a couple good bears on that hunt. Then there's the time my wife and I spent five days sitting in ground blinds in Zimbabwe, where not a single animal came to the water holes. The list goes on.

That said, I do respond to many questions over the course of a year on the gear I use. Be it email or in the many seminars I deliver, people are always curious about the gear I use and why I choose it.

Personally, I'm not much of a gadget guy, not like my wife in the kitchen. If there's something that will help make my hunts more successful, I'm all over it. At the same time, I can't be bought. I've been offered big money by some companies I turned down, either because I didn't believe in their product or their vision.

I'm not saying I don't work on a paid sponsorship level with some companies, I do. The companies I choose to align myself with create products I use and believe in. They craft items that help make me a better hunter and allow me to carry out my job in comfort, with confidence and with increased success.

Without these sponsors I wouldn't be able to make a career out of what I do. It's simple, really; hunting costs money. There are even overhead costs when filming TV shows where the hunts themselves are fully compensated by outfitters. Travel, lodging, tags, licenses, food and more are part of every hunt, and as many hunts as I go on each year, it takes the support of sponsors to help offset these expenses.

The Gear

Obviously, the bow is the most important tool in the world of bowhunting. True, I won't be caught dead in the spring bear or turkey woods without my ThermaCell. You won't find me on any physically demanding hunts without SportHill clothing on my body. And you know I'll be shooting Gold Tip arrows wherever I go. But if it came down to survival, tags can't be filled without a weapon, in this case, a bow.

Prior to connecting with BowTech I shot other brands of bows, and liked them. There are many fine bows on the market, and some good people within other bow companies, I just personally prefer BowTech bows. Because the factory is less than 30 minutes from my home has something to do with it. The more time I was invited to spend at BowTech, the more I learned about the intricacies of precision bow manufacturing and bow performance.

Being so closely connected with the many fine people at BowTech greatly increased my level of knowledge, quickly. Their Binary Cam series of bows undoubtedly took bow manufacturing to a whole new level, and the consistency, accuracy, comfort and overall performance of these bows are the best I've ever shot.

Every year I vow to keep my current bow and not be forced into using one of the brand new models. But every year BowTech keeps delivering new, cutting-edge bows I can't resist. Just when you think they can't develop anything better, they do. It's this aggressive push forward that appeals to me, along with the fact I've never had a single problem with any of the more than a dozen models of bows I've hunted with over the years.

When it comes to the technicalities of bowhunting, the number one question I receive is, "Why do you offset your vanes?" This concept was brought to my attention by the folks at BowTech around 2005. Their high-speed camera studies showed just how efficient this fletching system could be, and I've seen it proven time and again in the field.

I use 2-inch vanes, setting the first vane 1/2 to 3/4 of an inch down from the top of the arrow itself, from where the insert slips in. From there, offset the other two vanes about 1/2-inch from one another. I've found this setup to accomplish the following:

1. It provides 3-inches of "shadow" where, when you spin it, you can see that as the arrow rotates, there is plenty of vane being exposed so the arrow can accurately track. Some folks, in an effort to gain more "shadow" will offset their vanes 3/4 of an inch, which gives nearly 4-inches of shadow.

2. The vanes are low-profile enough that when traveling in a crosswind, they are hardly impacted. This is the biggest advantage I've found when hunting out West, where longer shots in often windy conditions are fairly common.

3. The arrow seems to stabilize quicker when shooting larger broadheads.

4. When using the rest to bring together both broadheads and field points, there is less movement required, saving time and effort.

My offset vane setup. I shoot the foremost vane on
top (top arrow), so the two trailing vanes can clear my fall-away rest.

That's it. Pretty straight forward and it works. I've taken animals at long distances and in winds I would have not even have shot at were it not for this setup.

As for other gear related items, what you see in the photos and on TV are what I choose to use. I'm after comfortable clothes meant for aggressive, athletic-style hunting so common out West. I need boots that won't let me down, no matter how rugged the terrain.

Sturdy, cut-on-impact broadheads (I'm not a fan of expandables on big game), a durable arrow and a fast, reliable bow are what excite me. Give me tough sites with small fiber optics, a consistent rest and a dependable release system and I'm set.

As for packs and other accessories, I'm always playing with them. There are some great packs on the market, so take the time to find one that fits your needs. Explore what works for you and your hunting style and use it with confidence.

My Philosophy

Speaking of confidence, I see this as the most important factor in successful bowhunting. Growing up I was always involved in athletics, from fourth grade and into college. Bowhunting, unlike any other form of hunting, is more like an athletic sport. Not only do you have to deal with the physical and mental aspects of rigorous hunts, but you have to perform flawlessly when it comes time to make the shot on an animal.

Heart pounding, muscles burning, delirious from lack of food and water, bowhunting can be hard on the body and mind. Then having to connect on a shot come crunch time, well, not everyone can do it. The people who routinely fill their archery tags are the ones who work at it.

I work out year-round. I lift weights, run, bike, hike and eat a balanced diet, all for the sake of keeping in shape for the hunt. I also shoot my bow year-round. Picking up a bow and shooting it a week before the season opens is one of the biggest detriments to the sport of bowhunting. There's no way an athlete can tune in their body's muscle memory, or their gear, in that short of time and expect success. Unfortunately, the animals and fellow bowhunters are the ones who suffer the wrath of such neglect.

Find a practice regimen that works for you and dedicate yourself to it. For me, I shoot alone in my backyard. For someone else, going to a pro shop shooting range or competing in 3D shoots is what works best.

If you get stuck, consult friends or a pro shop for help, but don't over-think things. I once hunted with the all-time homerun leader in major league baseball. He picked up a bow for the first time less than a year from when I hunted with him. He shot that thing better than anyone I'd ever seen. He could hit a golf ball at 80 yards every shot in the meanest crosswind, with broadheads.

I asked him what he thought about bowhunting. He went on to say that he loved it, and how easy it was because all you had to do was put the pin where you want it, hold steady and release. He made it sound so simple.

I've seen many people analyze and overanalyze aspects of bowhunting so much, they psych themselves out and loose their confidence. Find what works best for you and stick with it.

Take a fundamental free throw for instance. In the world of basketball, the free throw is the most basic of all shots. Yet, watch any NBA game and you'll see every player has their own style. None may appear even close to one another, and some are even downright terrible form, but they all have found what works best for them. They practice it and don't overanalyze it. When there's a problem, they recognize it and fix it.

My point is, when shooting your bow, develop a routine, stick with it and apply it with confidence. The more repetition you can gain, the more accurate you'll become and the more confidence you'll have.

Once in your groove, it's time to hunt. By this time, all the practice you've dedicated yourself to should make any shots in the field feel automatic. I don't think my way through every single step when it comes time to shooting an

Find a bow setup you like, develop a consistent shooting routine and have confidence in it. Having confidence in your equipment and your shooting ability are the most important elements to successful bowhunting.

animal. The only thing I want to be focusing on when it comes time to shoot is how the animal is behaving.

The ultimate indicator of whether or not I'm going to take the shot comes down to how the animal is acting. If he's nervous, I likely won't shoot. Then again, I know a bear or elk won't jump the string like a whitetail will. If the animal is calm and relaxed, then I take my time. Being in a rush is a big mistake I often see being made by hunters. If the wind is in your favor and the animal relaxed, take your time, keep your composure and do things right, for one shot is usually all you get on an animal.

Spending time in the field and observing wildlife is a valuable learning tool. Also, don't be afraid to be aggressive. One thing TV has done for me is forced me to do things I normally wouldn't do, all for the sake of getting a show in the can. I'm not talking unethical stuff here, rather aggressive and creative moves I would otherwise have been reluctant to attempt. If you make a mistake, so what, that's part of the learning curve; get over it, learn from it and move on.

Workout & Shooting Routines

Physically speaking, when it comes to hunting I strive to put myself in the best shape possible. Being in top physical–and mental–shape allows me to more efficiently go about my job. It increases my odds of success by allowing me to carry out tasks, meet demands and perform at levels above the norm.

Being in shape allows me to more thoroughly enjoy each hunt I go on. It's much more gratifying when I reach the top of a mountain and take in the captivating scenery with all my wits about me, rather than being physically beat and mentally exhausted when I get there. It also helps make me a better shot, and a better hunter, overall.

Hunting for a living means I have a very busy schedule. There is no off-season, which means I workout year-round. I can't afford to get out of shape, period. Because my time is so tight with not only hunting, but writing books and magazine articles, speaking, scouting, photography and more, I can only commit so many hours a day to working out.

Lifting weights is my top priority. I lift five days a week, six is preferred. I'll focus on my core, legs, upper body and arms, respectively. Of all the forms of exercise I do, nothing makes me a better bow shot than pumping iron. Fit legs and a strong core stabilize the entire frame, whereby allowing me to hold steady at full-draw, no matter what the angle. A solid upper body (chest, back and shoulders) greatly impacts my shooting accuracy, as does having arms that are in good shape. When I neglect weight training for any length of time, my shooting immediately suffers.

Bowhunting takes us places we may otherwise never get to see.

In addition to lifting weights, I incorporate a steady routine of cross-training at least five days a week. This is where I build my cardio', a very important part of my fitness program. I simply don't have the time to devote to long distance runs, so get my cardio-fix in other ways.

Short, intense runs of a mile or two, where I get my heart rate up, takes care of the running side of my workout. Routinely pushing my body on an air-resistance, stationary bike is one of the best, and most taxing, ways to increase my cardio'. An elliptical rowing machine is also a great alternative, as is mountain biking.

I'll also do intense calisthenics and cross-training workouts, like plyometrics. There are some great training programs on the market and it's easy finding one or two that fit your needs. The key is being disciplined enough to stick to a regular workout.

Personally, I don't have time to go to a gym and spend two hours every day. Instead, we put a weight room in our home. Here, I have a complete range of free-weights, including bench press, squat racks and more. This not only pushes me to workout every day possible, it also saves time from having to drive to the nearest gym and back, about 45 minutes per day. I encourage people to do what's necessary in order to be committed to consistently working out; for me, it's working out at home.

Overall, I'll devote one-and-a-half to two-hours a day to working out. At the end of each workout, my body is fatigued. I don't just go through the motions, I push my body as hard as possible. During the slow season, where I'm not in the field, I strive to build strength and endurance. During the hunting season, when my time is very tight and I'm on the road a great deal, I try to maintain my overall fitness levels.

As for actually shooting my bow, I also do that year-round. I don't have time to drive to a pro-shop and shoot or attend 3D shoots. I have a range set up in my backyard, where I can shoot any time. Again, do what's most feasible for you.

During the months of January and February I'm happy to shoot three times a week. In March, I'll increase my shooting frequency to four or five times a week, as spring hunting season is just around the corner. April through June marks spring hunting for bear and turkey, and usually an overseas trip, which means I better be ready.

In preparation for the fall hunting season–which begins in August for me–I'll try to shoot six days a week, starting in mid-June. I have targets set throughout my backyard from 30 to 100 yards, out. I'll shoot at various targets, from bags to blocks to 3D forms.

Within each practice session, sound repetition is critical. As with lifting weights, I'm careful not to get caught simply going through the motions. Every shot I make is mechanically correct. Concentration levels are high and I force myself to develop a consistent routine.

Once at full-draw, I check my anchor points first, followed by leveling my bubble. Next, I put the sightpin on the spot and try to hold it steady for three seconds. At the shot, my follow-through continues holding on the point of impact. When I hit the field, all this is automatic.

I shoot with both eyes open and continually breathe until the moment of the shot, so as not to tense-up. I'll practice from every position a shot might come from, including odd angles I encounter in rugged country. I make it a point to practice in all conditions; high winds, rain, excessive heat, low light, heavy shadows and more. I'll shoot anywhere from one to four dozen arrows a day, depending on how I feel.

I'll also practice with all my hunting gear on, pack included. This ensures no surprises when it comes time to shoot at an animal. I want to know how all my gear fits and what it feels like when I'm shooting.

If you wear a face-mask or gloves, practice shooting with them on. More times than not, I wear a glove on my left hand when shooting. I don't like wearing a glove on my right hand–my release hand–unless it's really cold, due to the loss of dexterity it causes. I wear one on my left hand as it, along with the bow itself, serve as cover. When holding the bow up, the limbs, riser, string, cables, quiver, arrows and gloved hand, all help breakup my outline. Hiding behind my bow has allowed me to arrow many approaching elk, deer and bear over the years.

These are some workout and shooting tips that have helped me find consistent success, no matter where in the world I'm hunting. Do what you can to strive to be the best you can be. I'm never content with "good enough," I'm always pushing myself to improve. I owe it to myself, the animals and fellow hunters.

Ultimately, we're all in the woods because we choose to be there. Hunting, no matter what the form, is a sport of choice and we need to support one another, period. It pains me every time I hear of trail cameras or treestands being stolen, or worse yet, one faction of hunters bashing another. Whether a person hunts with bow or gun, we're a small fraternity and we need to stick together. As long as it's legal and ethical, we should support it.

Hunting is a sport, but it's not a competition to see who can score the most points. Hunting is about preparing one's self for a challenging outdoor experience, knowing all you possibly can about the animals you pursue, and being able to do all that's necessary to ethically close the deal with a well-placed shot. Having highly nutritious meat to subsist on, and perhaps a trophy-class animal to admire, are just two of the benefits that come from hunting.

As I've said before, were it not for hunting I'd not be compelled to travel the world just to see what's out there. Hunting takes me places I'd otherwise never go. It pushes me to the limits, just like those college football days when enduring daily-doubles in 100° forced me to reach deep within myself to get the job done.

For me, the ultimate rush in bowhunting is connecting with a single, well-placed shot on an animal after a strategic stalk. But the biggest reward comes in reliving it for fellow sportsmen and women through writing and TV. It's my hope to educate and motivate all hunters to get out and experience the excitement I've been fortunate to.

Every day I'm out there I give thanks to God for allowing me the wonderful opportunities which have come my way. Bowhunting does that to a person, it connects us with the land, the animals and our Creator on levels we'd otherwise never know. We, as hunters, are very blessed to have what we do, and it's our responsibility to advocate ethical hunting and convey our passions to future generations of fellow hunters so they can one day live the dream.